P9-CJX-451

Musically Speaking

To Lisa
best wishes!
Dr. Ruth K. Westheimer

Personal Takes

An occasional series of short books in which noted critics write about the persistent hold particular writers, artists, or cultural phenomena have had on their imaginations.

Musically Speaking

A Life Through Song

Dr. Ruth K. Westheimer

UNIVERSITY OF PENNSYLVANIA PRESS
Philadelphia

Copyright © 2003 University of Pennsylvania Press
All rights reserved
Printed in the United States of America on acid-free paper

10 9 8 7 6 5 4 3

Published by
University of Pennsylvania Press
Philadelphia, Pennsylvania 19104-4011

Library of Congress Cataloging-in-Publication Data

Westheimer, Ruth K. (Ruth Karola), 1928–
Musically speaking : a life through song / Ruth K. Westheimer.
p. cm. – (Personal takes)
Contents: Dear bird, fly on – Thoughts are free – Our hope is not lost – Je ne regrette rien – If I can make it there.
ISBN 0-8122-3746-3 (cloth : alk. paper)
1. Music, Influence of. 2. Sex therapists–United States–Biography. 3. Westheimer, Ruth K. (Ruth Karola), 1928–. I. Title. II. Series.
ML3920.W33 2003
616.85'83'0092–dc21 2003053128
[B]

Permission has kindly been granted to reprint lyrics from the following. From "You Are My Sunshine," by Jimmie Davis. Copyright © 1940 by Peer International Corporation. Copyright © renewed. International rights secured. Used by permission. All rights reserved. From "I'm Gonna Wash That Man Right Outa My Hair," by Richard Rodgers and Oscar Hammerstein II. Copyright © 1949 by Richard Rodgers and Oscar Hammerstein II. Copyright renewed. Williamson Music owner of publication and allied rights throughout the world. International copyright secured. All rights reserved. Used by permission. From "Leaving on a Jet Plane." Words and music by John Denver. Copyright © 1967; renewed 1995 Cherry Lane Music Publishing Company, Inc. (ASCAP) and DreamWorks Songs (ASCAP). Rights for DreamWorks Songs administered by Cherry Lane Music Publishing Company, Inc. International copyright secured. All rights reserved. From the song "Little Boxes." Words and music by Malvina Reynolds. © copyright 1962 Schroder Music Co. (ASCAP). Renewed 1990. Used by permission. All rights reserved. From "The Music of the Night" from *The Phantom of the Opera*. Music: Andrew Lloyd Webber. Lyrics: Charles Hart. Additional lyrics: Richard Stilgoe. © copyright 1986 The Really Useful Group Ltd., London. All rights reserved. International copyright secured. From "No Time at All," by Stephen Schwartz. © 1972 (renewed) Stephen Schwartz. All rights for the world administered by EMI Mills Music, Inc. and Jobete Music Co., Inc. All rights reserved. Used by permission. Warner Bros. Publications U.S. Inc., Miami, FL 33014. From "Two Kinds of Seagulls." Music and lyrics by John Forster; additional lyrics by Tom Chapin. © 1990 by Limousine Music Co. (ASCAP) and The Last Music Co. (ASCAP). All rights reserved.

As songs were your laws unto me wherever I wandered.
—Psalm 119:54

Contents

Overture

I am, and have always been, the first to admit: I cannot carry a tune. I have known this at least since I was ten years old. Until that time, my father, mother, and grandmother had spared me from any suggestion that I might be deficient as a singer. This—and so much else—changed once I left our loving home in Frankfurt am Main, Germany, for the Swiss children's home in which I would live from the ages of ten to fifteen. Singing in the choir at the Swiss home, I became well aware of my limitations, and I made sure to sing very softly, so I wouldn't ruin the beautiful sounds everybody else was making.

One of my first real jobs as an adult was as a kindergarten teacher, in Paris, in the early 1950s. Kindergarten teachers *have* to sing, of course, and my supervisors were very concerned about my limitations. It was a Jewish school, and they brought in a retired cantor to try to train my voice. After two or three lessons, he gave up. I remember him saying, "You'll be a great kindergarten teacher, but you'll never sing." I eventually learned how to play simple melodies on the recorder instead.

In recent years, here in the United States, I've gotten to know a man named Matthew Lazar, a conductor and arranger. We've often spoken about my vocal limitations. I once gave him a pillow embroidered with the words "The woods would be very silent if no birds sang there except those who sang best." Matthew is a brave man, and he insists *everybody* can sing. He's given me some instruction, and even though I will still sing only when I'm alone in the car or my apartment, I have to say that he did a better job with me than the cantor in Paris.

I am what is charitably called an "inaccurate" singer. Less sensitively, people like me are deemed "tone deaf." We are "problem-" or "nonsingers," branded as "droners" and "pitch deficient," "uncertain," or simply "out of tune." The consensus of scholars who have studied us is that the problem might lie in one of three areas: our hearing or monitoring of ourselves while singing, the way in which we remember the music we intend to sing, or our failure to reproduce this remembered melody. Various methods have actually been shown to be effective in improving the abilities of inaccurate young singers. One technique is for a teacher to hold the child's face in his or her hands while singing a pattern the child has been told to repeat. Instructing children to place their hands over their ears in self-monitoring can also work, and so can having them sing the syllable "loo," because words can be distracting. The use of echo singing exercises can improve tonal memory, as can vocal inflection exercises involving imitation of sounds like the wind, sirens, and animal sounds. Exercises that promote correct posture and breathing are important.* Unfortunately none of these

*Moira Szabo, "Children's Inaccurate Singing: Selected Contributing Factors," *General Music Today* 4 (Spring 2001): 4–9.

were tried on me, and I'm afraid it's too late to start now. But that's OK; I'm comfortable with my limitations.

The fact is, aside from being a poor singer, I don't really like music. Let me immediately clarify that statement: I don't like music as an *accompaniment* to other activities. My husband Fred, who died six years ago, always went around our apartment turning the radio on; I went around turning it off. He seemed to live and breathe music. He loved Russian folk songs and, indeed, Russian music of all kinds (which is strange, considering that he was of German Jewish extraction, spent some of his childhood in Portugal, and never went to Russia), protest songs like "Joe Hill" and "We Shall Overcome," religious melodies, oratorios like *Carmina Burana*, fados from Portugal (his parents moved there in 1938 and stayed there even after Fred came to this country in 1941)—everything, it seemed. Actually, one of the first things that attracted me to him when we met in 1961 was that he played Jewish folk songs on his harmonica. (He also played the guitar, and when we first started going out, he left his guitar at another woman's house. To prevent him from going back and getting it, I bought him a *new* guitar. Even though $28 was a fortune for me in those days, it turned out to be the best money I ever spent.) At one point, long after we were married, he decided he wanted to take piano lessons. I made a deal with him: I would pay for the lessons, on the condition that I would never have to listen to him practice.

I cannot stand to have music on when I am reading, writing, when I just want to sit quietly, or when I am trying to have a conversation. I know there is a long tradition of *Tafelmusik*, or table music, but it is not for me. If you are listening to music, even with one ear, you are not using all your concentration and ability to connect with the person nearby. If I am seated next to someone in whom I am interested, whom I want to get to know, to share thoughts and ideas with, music is a terrible distraction. One of the great pleasures of my life is getting massages but *not* with that terrible New Age massage music. I always insist that the masseur turn it off (unless he needs it). And, if you must know, I do not like music during sex, either. If you need music in moments like these, well . . .

And yet.

These days, I find myself drawn to music as I never have been before. Fred's death has something to do with this, I think. After he had his first stroke, in 1996, Michael Kruk, the cantor from our synagogue, came to visit him in the intensive care unit. Michael was born in Russia, where he sang in the Red Army chorus, and lived in Israel before coming to this country; he is a trained opera singer. You can hear the sound of all these places and traditions in his singing. When he sings the "Shema," the most important prayer in the Jewish religion ("Hear O Israel, the Lord our God, the Lord is One"), it sounds to me like the heavens have to open up to hear his voice. And during Friday night services, he sings—beautifully—many of the melodies I remember from my childhood years in Frankfurt. In the hospital, Michael sang "Katusha," a Russian folk song about a young woman in wartime who sings to her boyfriend that she is waiting for him to come back home to her. He sang it almost in slow motion, so that Fred would understand exactly what he was singing, and it worked: Fred said later that he remembered the music. A year later Fred had another stroke and did not recover. At his memorial ceremony, I asked Michael to sing "Katusha" again. At first he said he didn't think he could do it, but I persisted, and he agreed. He sang it very softly, the way he did in the hospital, and every one of the six hundred people who were there will always remember it. His efforts brought home for me the power of music to heal and to comfort. Michael's singing didn't make my pain go away, but for a moment, I could lose it. Music can take you away from present difficulties, transport you to a happier time in the past.

But music can be very complicated for me. One melody that has followed me through my life is the refrain of Josef Haydn's String Quartet in C Major, composed in 1797. It is better known as the melody of "Das Lied der Deutschen"–and still better known by its opening words, "Deutschland, Deutschland, über alles"–which became the German national anthem in 1922, six years before I was born in Frankfurt am Main. My grandmother used to take me to the Palmengarten, the botanical garden in the West End of Frankfurt, where she would meet her sister and friends, who had all brought *their* grandchildren. As is still the case in parks all over Europe, there was a band shell. Music was always around, and we would hear waltzes, oom-pah music, and string ensembles. I am sure that I first heard "Das Lied der Deutschen" there with her, played from the bandstand. Today, whenever I hear the song, it conjures up images I know more from photographs and films, of Nazis marching through the streets. Yet I cannot banish the melody from my mind just for this. It plays from a clock I have hanging on the wall, and every now and then I catch myself humming the tune. I stop myself—but then I tell myself to go right on. For what did Haydn know of Nazism, and why should the Nazis take Haydn, and the memory of my grandmother, away from me?

I lost everything that was dear and important to me in my childhood, and in order not to live in a vacuum, in order to feel the ground beneath my feet, I have to keep the memories of

these things alive. The stories that were read to me as a child, the songs that were sung probably take the place of the family histories I would have heard throughout my childhood and adolescence. Family life ended abruptly for me at the age of ten. The melodies and the words of the songs I knew provide a link with the past forever.

There is another cantor I know and admire, Joseph Malovany, born in Israel but now living in New York. He has an extraordinary voice and a stage presence to match. When he sings in synagogue or performs as he did the other evening at Lincoln Center, in a benefit for a Jerusalem hospital, I invariably find myself moved to tears. And these are tears of joy and sadness combined. For a few moments, his songs restore the lost old world to me and remind me anew of just how important and steadying a force tradition has always been for me. When he switches to more modern and up-tempo Israeli pieces, my love for that land comes rushing back. "If I Forget Thee, O Jerusalem," "You Shall Know No More War," "He Who Brought Us to This Time": these songs seem to trace the trajectory of my life.

Since Fred's death, music has been more a part of my life than it has been at any time since my youth. And not only in the theater and the concert hall. When I'm alone, as I am so much more often these days, I find myself singing, sometimes in my head, sometimes out loud. Very often, the songs carry me back to times that are precious to me for their happiness. Sometimes, they enable me to revisit the most sorrowful things I have experienced. I am a *Jecke*—a German Jew—and you must trust me that we tend to keep our emotions contained. A *Jecke* doesn't cry. These visits to the past are safe, however, because I have control over when to stop a certain melody in my head, when to substitute it with another, or when to rewrite the words to make them more acceptable.

When I am on the ski slopes, I am always singing an internal song. This, I should point out, is a matter of self-preservation rather than aesthetics. I find that if I think about papers I have to write or the state of the world, I fall down. If I sing, I can stay in rhythm and make the proper bends. I always sing the same song on the slopes: a Hebrew song with words by the Russian Jewish poet Saul Tchernikhovski translated as "Laugh, laugh about the dreams that I, the dreamer, tell." I wasn't even aware I was singing it until one day I was skiing with my daughter, Miriam, and she asked me what I was singing. Only then did I realize I was singing at all.

I learned that song more than fifty years ago. And that is significant. The songs that fill my interior landscape are the old ones. No rock and roll, no modern classical pieces, none of the show tunes that I heard after coming to the United States in 1956. No, they are the songs of my youth—in Frankfurt am Main, in Switzerland, in Palestine and then Israel, and a little bit in France. I will find myself singing a Zionist song I learned in Switzerland whose words go,

> Every person in this world
> Has his own country. . . .
> Only one people in the world
> Has no homeland of their own,
> And every day there stands before them
> The eternal Jewish question,
> "Whither, Jew?
> Who in the world will take you?"

When I'm sad about not having a companion, I will sing "Das verlassene Mägdlein" ("The Abandoned Maiden"), a German song I have carried with me for most of my life:

> Early, when the roosters crow,
> Before the stars have disappeared,
> I have to stand at the hearth
> I have to kindle the fire. . . .
> This is how the day arrives,
> I wish it would go away.

The truth is, I have always hummed or sung these songs, but always sotto voce when someone else is around.

Music, I have come to realize, is for me a kind of *Leitfaden*, a golden thread running through my life. It has been a vitally important accompaniment to me, without my having thought much about it. Like a silent partner and friend, music has given me emotional sustenance and an inner home. It has helped maintain a connection to the past that otherwise might have been severed by catastrophe and time. I am often asked–indeed, I often wonder myself–why it is that I should always have had such joie de vivre in the face of the losses and dislocations I had to endure in the early years of my life. The answer I always gave was that the warmth and security of my early childhood socialization had a remarkable power and influence. This is certainly true. But now I have realized that there is another part to the answer. And that is music.

CHAPTER ONE

Dear bird, fly on

I was born in 1928 in Frankfurt am Main—Frankfurt on the Main River—in Germany. My childhood, what little of it I had, was by any measure a happy one. My father sold notions for a living, and the family was comfortable but by no means wealthy. We—my parents, my grandmother, and me, the only child—lived in a ground-floor, four-room apartment on Brahmsstrasse (all the streets in the neighborhood were named after composers—a coincidence, given the subject of this book, but also an indication of the respect Frankfurt and Germany accorded music and the men who created it). I loved going to school, and I did well enough that at the beginning of the fifth grade, I was selected to enter the *Sexta*, the first part of the gymnasium, or high school. One of my favorite memories is of a game we played at recess. The girls all held hands and walked in a circle around another girl, who acted out the story of a little princess who at first was sad and cried but then met Prince Charming. All the while everybody else sang songs about her story. So you see that love and romance—and a sense of community—were all part of my life from a very early age.

I remember participating in another such play-song with the neighborhood children–Christian and Jew–on Brahmsstrasse. We would stand in a circle, and when you were "it," you would sing, "Brüderlein, komm, tanz mit mir" ("Little boy, come dance with me"), and go over to a boy and take him by the hand. I especially loved that part!

That song is still in my head today, and so are a number of other simple German songs. The first song I ever learned, I think, was "Backe, backe Kuchen" ("Bake, bake a cake"), a children's song where you clap your hands to the rhythm. "Zeigt hier eure Füsschen" ("Show your feet and look at the washerwoman") was another one of those games where we stood in a circle and acted out a story with song and movements. I don't know why children in today's world don't seem to be taught these songs as much as we were. They teach not only coordination and movement but also cooperation, how to act in unison, and how to be attentive and disciplined depending on what the words tell you to do.

My dear friend Ilse Wyler, who spent the years of World War II with me in a children's home in Switzerland–more about that later–and who now lives near Zurich, recently mailed me an old book of German children's songs. Paging through it, I found that a remarkable number of the songs came back to me instantly, as if it were yesterday that I was singing them. Songs such as "Hopp, hopp, hopp" ("Hop, hop, little horse, run"), "Es klappert die Mühle am rauschenden Bach" ("The mill standing at a small river makes the noise clip clop clip clop"), "Der Kuckuck und der Esel" (wherein the cuckoo and the donkey quarrel about who sings the best during the lovely days of May), "Fuchs, du hast die

Gans gestohlen" ("Fox, you stole the goose / Return her or the hunter will get you with his rifle"), and "Ein Männlein steht im Walde" ("A little man stands in the woods alone and quiet") are all suddenly alive for me again. They are all old folk songs, or melodies composed in the nineteenth century (mostly in the early nineteenth century), and here I am, sitting a continent away in the early years of the twenty-first century, still humming them and finding myself immediately transported to the streets of Frankfurt more than six decades ago. It is a remarkable demonstration of the power of music and song to overcome time, space, and history.

I remember quite a few German lullabies from my childhood: Brahms's "Lullaby," of course, which my parents and grandmother must have sung to me from the time I was a baby; "Weißt du, wieviel Sternlein stehen" ("Do you know how many stars are in the blue canopy of sky?"), "Schlaf, Kindlein, schlaf" ("Sleep, little child, sleep"), and another delightful lullaby, "Die Blümelein, sie schlafen" ("The flowers, they sleep in the moonlight. . . . / The blossoming tree quivers, it whispers as if in a dream, / 'Sleep, sleep my little child.'"). I sang that lullaby—which has a melody written by Heinrich Isaak back in 1490—to my children. And maybe I mangled the melody, but I felt—and still feel—the sweetness of it in my bones.

The psychoanalyst Theodor Reik once wrote an entire book, called *The Haunting Melody*, about the uncanny way a piece of music—even just a line of a song—will stay with us over decades and decades, popping into the mind when we least expect it, sometimes sliding in stealthily, but sometimes packing a sizable emotional wallop. "Nothing that passes through the intellect, such as a line of poetry or the memory of a work of art, a fragrance or a smell, can haunt us with the same intensity or cause us to react with the same vigor," he writes,* and he cites Proust's *Remembrance of Things Past*, where Swann is haunted by a "little phrase" (*la petite phrase*) from a piano and violin sonata. It works much like the more famous Madeleine cookie in the same novel: every time he hears it, it powerfully and ineffably evokes the image of his lover Odette. I like the image, though for me the songs of my childhood are more like pictures in a photograph album than a plate of cookies. When a piece of music is meaningful to me, it anchors the memory of not just the people or places with which I associate it but the feelings as well, even feelings of hopelessness and despair.

Two songs from my early childhood that would have meanings I could not foresee are "Hänschen klein" and "Kommt ein Vogel geflogen." Both sing of children separated from their parents, and I guess I respond more to the lyrics than to their lilting music. "Hänschen klein," or "Little Hans," is a folk melody with words supplied by the nineteenth-century writer Franz Wiedemann. These go,

> Little Hans
> Went alone
> Into the wide world,

*Theodor Reik, *The Haunting Melody: Psychoanalytic Experiences in Life and Music* (New York: Farrar, Straus & Cudahy, 1953), p. 27.

Looking good,
Hat and stick in hand,
In a happy mood.
But his mamma cried so much,
Because she did not have little Hans any more.
So he reconsidered,
That child,
And returned home promptly.
"Dear Mom,
I've returned . . .
And from now on I'll stay here
And never leave you again."

(Interestingly, Freud gave one of his most famous case studies, published in 1909, the name "Little Hans." I have no way of knowing if he had the song in mind, but I like to think he did.)

Even more poignant when I look back on it is "Kommt ein Vogel geflogen," or "A Bird Comes Flying to Me." Written in 1822, with lyrics by Adolf Bäuerle and music by Wenzel Müller, the words go like this:

A bird comes flying to me,
Sits on my foot,
Has a note in his beak,
A greeting from my mother.
Dear bird, fly on.
Take my greetings with you and a kiss
Since I can't join you.
I must remain here.

Shortly, I would be separated from my parents through war and I would be living in the children's home in Switzerland, not sure if I would ever see my family again (I would not). It may seem that, with their sentimental messages of family and loneliness, these two songs would have been too much to bear. But the fact remains that I sang them again and again and, somehow, took some comfort from them. And music does have this capacity to help us address our emotions, some of them happy, some of them sad, some of them indescribable in words. It may seem an odd comparison, perhaps, but I wonder if for me, those simple German songs were not somehow the equivalent of the blues for American blacks: a way to confront my unhappiness and loneliness and, for a moment at least, overcome them.

In my girlhood home in Frankfurt, we had no piano, no phonograph, and while I do remember a vacuum tube radio, I don't remember music coming out of it. So I imagine that my grandmother, Selma, my father's mother, must have sung all these songs to me. Unlike my mother and father, who were both thin, she was rather heavy (save for the thin white hair worn in a bun on top of her head). And also unlike my mother and father, who were quiet sorts, she was very talkative, and I have always needed people to talk to. My grandmother was a very important person in my childhood.

She didn't sing any of the Yiddish songs that many people think of nostalgically as Jewish music; nor was the instrumental klezmer music that has become so popular in recent years ever a part of my childhood. This all originated in eastern

Europe or among eastern European Jews—and we *Jeckes* (as German Jews are known) felt ourselves quite apart from that. It was only after I emigrated to Palestine, years later, that I came to know—and love—this music, some of it so joyous, some so melancholy. And I have no memory from Frankfurt of the popular German songs of the day—some so similar, if you hear them now, to American music of the thirties—or of the artists who made them famous. Perhaps I was simply too young to take notice, or perhaps my parents and grandmother were trying to protect me from what was going on in Germany outside the nurturing cocoon of our home.

It was a very Jewish environment in which I lived, those first ten and a half years in Frankfurt, at home and at school, and at sleep-away camp during the summers. The only Christian adult I consciously knew was Frau Luft, the one-armed woman who would come to our house every Shabbos to light the stove. It is strange, then, that I remember with fondness quite a few Christmas songs. How did I know them? I don't know. I recall "O du fröhliche" ("A Wonderful Messenger") and "Ihr Kinderlein, kommet" ("Oh, children, come you all, / Come to the manger in Bethlehem"), and certainly "Silent Night" (in German it is "Stille Nacht, heilige Nacht"), written in 1818 by Franz Gruber and Joseph Mohr. I obviously did not respond to the description of the baby Jesus but to the image of everyone sleeping in a deep and profound peace and quiet. Perhaps my favorite of the Christmas carols is "O Tannenbaum," one that's also familiar in America, as I discovered when I came here in the 1950s. Needless to say, we didn't have a Christmas tree in our apartment, but the lyrics, written in 1820 by Joachim Zarnack and Ernst Anschütz to a folk melody, talk about how faithful the pine needles are in all the seasons of the year, and this resonated with me. Those lyrics carry a lesson about hope and steadfastness—although I guess it may seem odd that it was to a Christmas song that I kept returning for the strength I needed during the difficult years of my adolescence and early adulthood.

What other musical memories do I have from childhood? When I think back to my visits to the Palmengarten with my grandmother, a soundtrack of band music plays, but I recall the feeling of excitement and well-being more than the specific tunes. I have an image, too, of being alone somewhere in downtown Frankfurt standing in the middle of a ring of people; they are not my school friends playing one of our circle games but tall and majestic Abyssinians singing and dancing around me, and I don't know what I am expected to do, how I am to emerge. Did this really happen? It seems unlikely, not the least because I would not have been downtown on my own, yet the memory is quite vivid, and I don't think it was a dream.

Clearer are the recollections of peddlers and musicians who would come into the courtyard of our apartment building from time to time. My grandmother would give me a few coins to wrap up in a scrap of paper, and I would rush to the window with delight, tossing down the money to them as they sang. One of their songs in particular stuck in my memory:

Die Tyroler sind lustig,
Die Tyroler sind froh.

Sie haben kein Essen,
Sie schlafen auf Stroh.

(The Tyroleans are merry, / The Tyroleans are gay. / They have nothing to eat, / They sleep on straw.)*

How peculiar, I thought, that people would sleep on straw instead of in a proper bed, that they could be so good humored without a grandmother, mother, and father to keep them well fed and warm. How could I know that I would soon be more like the Tyroleans in the song than I could ever have imagined?

We were Orthodox Jews, and it was in synagogue that I was exposed most regularly to music. Every Friday evening my father would take me to shul, not to the enormous synagogue on Börnestrasse, to which we belonged, but to the smaller one attached to the old-age and nursing home on Gagernstrasse, where his presence would help ensure that there would be a minyan, the group of ten men over the age of bar mitzvah, necessary for any prayer to take place. Jews are not permitted to carry money on the Sabbath, but he always made sure there was just enough change in his vest pocket to buy me an ice cream cone on the way there, before the sun had gone down. It was unusual that my father should have taken me to synagogue,

*In fact, my memory of the song is likely faulty, as I discovered in the process of writing this book. It is not, as I have gone through life thinking, that the Tyroleans go without food. In the printed versions of the lyric I have found, the third line reads, "Sie versaufen das Bettzeug" ("They drink away their bedding"). Such irresponsible behavior was clearly outside my frame of reference.

because the tradition was for the men to go and the women to stay home and prepare for dinner. But there was no son in the family, and therefore I went along with him. Then, and also when we went to Saturday morning services, because I was just a child, I was allowed to sit in the men's section with him, instead of being relegated to the women's section upstairs. Maybe it had to do with being up close, but in any case, the music of the services still plays in my head.

I remember the song welcoming the Sabbath: "Lechah Dodi Likrat Kalah Penei Shabbat Nekabela." The words talk about the Sabbath being like a bride, and at the end of the song, everybody turns to the door as if the "bride" were really about to walk in (I was always especially excited by this part). And of course the "Shema," the most beautiful liturgical melody, and one of the holiest, and the "Kaddish," the prayer for the dead, which is really more sing-song than melodic. There was special music on Saturday morning as well. When the Torah is taken out, the congregation sings "Zot Hatorah Asher"–"This is the Torah that God told you to observe." That joyous and majestic melody is very much in my head–when I hear it, I know I come from Frankfurt am Main, from an Orthodox traditional background.

The synagogue was the place for prayers, but the place where we really sang together was at Friday night Shabbos dinner with my father, mother, and grandmother. After we gathered at the table, we would sing "Shalom Aleichem"–"Peace be to you, O ministering angels, messengers of the Most High, the supreme King of Kings." When we sang, we understood that the worries of the week, the concerns about making a living and what the future would bring, had to be put on hold. Then came my favorite song, which the husband sings to the wife while everyone in the room stands up, "Eshet Chayil," or "Woman of Valor." The words go, "Who can find a woman of valor? There are many good women out there who do good things, but you are the best of them all." I have always felt, and I still tell lecture audiences today, that these are the most sexually arousing words it would ever be possible for a man to say to a woman. As a matter of fact, I wear a pendant with these words inscribed.

Before "Eshet Chayil," the women would light the candles and say the appropriate blessing. Next was "Yevarechecha Hashem" ("May God Bless You"); the children–in my family, just me–get blessed by the father and mother. One of my favorite melodies was Louis Lewandowski's "Veshamru B'nai Yisrael": "The children of Israel shall keep the Sabbath, observing the Sabbath in every generation as a covenant for all time. It is a sign forever, between Me and the people of Israel, for in six days the eternal God made heaven and earth, and on the seventh day He rested from His labors." After the food we sang the "Shir Hamaalot," a song of praise, and then the "Benschen," the blessing in which everyone has to participate, so they won't fall asleep.

It's not surprising that music, with its power to express and elicit joy, reflection, emotion, and sometimes transcendence, would play a part in almost all religions. For Jews, perhaps because of the dislocations and disasters we have been subject to throughout our history, the relationship to music has been rather an ambivalent one, but certainly, in the Old Testament, there are numerous references to its power. In Exodus 15:20, we read that Moses' sister, Miriam, led the Hebrew women to a location outside the desert encampment where they sang and danced to celebrate the crossing of the Red Sea. At Mt. Sinai, before the giving of the Ten Commandments, the Lord tells Moses, "When the trumpet sounds a long blast, they shall come up to the mountain." That, of course, is the shofar, the ram's horn which we still hear today on Rosh Hashanah. Later, the Lord tells Moses that his brother, Aaron, shall be a priest and that Aaron's robe should in itself be a kind of instrument: "On its skirts you shall make pomegranates of blue and purple and scarlet stuff, around its skirts, with bells of gold between them, a golden bell and a pomegranate. . . . And it shall be upon Aaron when he ministers, and its sound shall be heard when he goes into the holy place before the Lord and when he comes out, lest he die." The prophet Samuel, in anointing Saul king, tells him how music can be a means of stimulating ecstatic states: "as you come to the city, you will meet a band of prophets coming down from the high place with harp, tambourine, flute, and lyre before them, prophesying. Then the spirit of the Lord will come mightily upon you, and you shall prophesy with them and be turned into another man." The Book of Samuel also tells us that King Saul's torments were healed when the young David played the lyre for him: "And whenever the evil spirit from God was upon Saul, David took the lyre and played it with his hand; so Saul was refreshed, and was well, and the evil spirit departed from him." (Of course, Saul and David later had their problems, but that is a different story.)

We have no way of knowing what any of it really sounded like, but we do know that in ancient Israel, music had a central role in religious life. When the ark was brought to the Temple in Jerusalem, "David and all Israel were making merry before God with all their might, with song and lyres and harps and tambourines and cymbals and trumpets." And music was important in worship as well, for example, as an accompaniment to the burnt offerings: "And when the burnt offering began, the song to the Lord began also, and the trumpets, accompanied by the instruments of David king of Israel. The whole assembly worshiped, and the singers sang, and the trumpeters sounded; all this continued until the burnt offering was finished." The singers and musicians were the Levites, members of the tribe of Levi who inherited the possession and lore of the sacred instruments and music.

David—clearly a musical genius—was traditionally known as the author of the songs of the service, that is, the Psalms. We do not know the melody of the Psalms, but we have their words, as collected in the Book of Psalms, and we can gather something of how the music sounded. As Judith Kaplan Eisenstein writes in her *Heritage of Music*, "Some of the psalms have headings which tell us they were to be sung to certain popular tunes of the day, 'To the Lilies of the Sharon,' 'To the Morning Star,' and others." The titles of others, such as "To the Instrument of Ten Strings," give a clear clue to the accompaniment.*

*See Judith Kaplan Eisenstein, *Heritage of Music: The Music of the Jewish People* (New York: Union of American Hebrew Congregations, 1972), 12.

David's son, King Solomon, is considered to be the author of "Shir Hashirim" ("The Song of Songs"), and to my mind it is one of the most beautiful love songs ever written. As it is included in the Bible, it has sometimes been interpreted as an expression of love between God and the people of Israel, and I'm in no position to dispute that. Not surprisingly, though, given my professional interests, I have a different view, and given the frequency with which it is recited at weddings, I'm not alone. Listen to how Solomon speaks of the close connections between music, sex, and love:

Behold the winter is past,
The rain is over and gone,
The flowers appear on the earth,
The time of singing is come,
And the voice of the turtle dove is heard in the land.

What I wouldn't give to hear the original melody!

The liturgy of the First Temple consisted mainly of psalms attributed to David and his musicians. They were sung, in melodies and configurations that are now lost to us, but there is no question that beautiful sounds filled the Temple before its destruction by the Babylonians in 586 B.C.E. We know a little more about the music in the Second Temple: according to the Mishnah, the collection of Jewish law that was codified in the third century C.E., there was a choir consisting of at least twelve Levites and a substantial orchestra. The priest blew at least two trumpets and signaled the start of worship with an instrument called a *magrefah*.

Everything changed in 70 C.E., when the Roman army under Titus destroyed the Second Temple. From that point on, music became much less prevalent in Jewish religious life. No instruments were allowed in the synagogue except for the shofar on Rosh Hashanah, so that liturgical music became purely vocal (instrumental music has reemerged only recently, historically speaking, in the Reconstructionist and Reform movements). Also, many prohibitions against secular music were put into place. One reason for the curtailing of music was that the Jewish people were in mourning for the destruction of the Temple, and joyous melodies were unseemly; another was that Gentile worship was marked by music, and the Jews did not want to be seen as imitating it.

But another factor was a kind of Puritanism (if I may say so) that could be found in Jewish texts even before the destruction of the Temple and that was more and more in evidence afterward. The Old Testament tells us a lot about the importance of music in secular life. There are descriptions of music playing at a farewell ceremony, at the digging of a well, at a celebration of victory, and at the harvesting of grapes. This is all to the good. Already, though, music is sometimes associated with the corruption of the rich, and Isaiah specifically links it with harlotry: "Take a harp, go about the city, O forgotten harlot! Make sweet melody, sing many songs, that you may be remembered."

In rabbinical writings, one begins to find many statements to the effect that music leads to promiscuity. According to one Talmudic source, "A woman's voice is indecency." Another supports this with chapter and verse: "How was Solomon, the wisest man in the world, misled by his wives in the worship of idols? By means of music. The daughter of Pharaoh, Solomon's favorite wife, brought with her a thousand different kinds of musical instruments, and ordered that they be played for Solomon, saying, 'Thus do we play for Osiris and thus for Ophais.' Solomon was charmed, and his senses were beguiled." In the Temple, men and women were separated, and the women were not permitted to sing, except, perhaps in an auxiliary "court of women." To our modern sensibilities, this seems terribly wrong and unfair. And yet one cannot simply write it off to ancient beliefs, for the attitude continued down through the centuries, certainly up to my experience as a girl, and in Orthodox synagogues even until today.

I don't want to simplify things too much, though. One post-Diaspora Jewish tradition where music played an important and positive role was in the mysticism and messianism of the Kabbalah. The strains were woven into the *Zohar*, the thirteenth-century text so central to the study of Kabbalah, where music is emphasized as a means to a kind of religious transcendence and ecstasy. The *Zohar* quotes the second-century rabbi Simeon bar Yohai: "Hearken well to the music of the spheres. There are choirs of angels intoning the music and harmony of the spheres. The prophets, the singers, the seers, and the mystics, when they feel themselves possessed of the Divine Spirit . . . , are able to disengage themselves from this material world and to vision themselves climbing to the heights of music of this Divine melody." The ultrareligious Hasidic movement, which began in the sixteenth century and reached its full flowering at the turn of the nineteenth century, taught that wordless singing and dancing could bring one close to mystical rapture. At every significant occasion, in the synagogue or elsewhere, special songs were sung, and one branch of Hasidism, the Chabad, even developed a series of six spiritual levels of song and dance. As you ascended from one to another, higher and higher levels of spirituality were achieved, leading up to *hitpashtut hagashmiyut* (soul as disembodied spirit).*

As a little girl in the Frankfurt synagogue, I was witnessing the fruits of significant changes regarding music and the liturgy, though I didn't know it at the time. The so-called Emancipation of European Jews, in the eighteenth and nineteenth centuries, brought on new and freer ways of thinking, influenced by the Enlightenment, that were reflected in synagogue practices. Most notably, the Reform movement, which took hold in Germany in the early nineteenth century, had substituted German prayers for the traditional ones in Hebrew, abolished the chanting of the Scripture, and, most dramatically, introduced the organ into the synagogue and reduced the role of the traditional cantor, or hazan. Our family was Orthodox, but the Reform movement definitely had an effect on the way we worshiped. Musically, this involved the compositions and innovations of Saloman Sulzer (1804–90) and Louis Lewandowski (1821–94).

Sulzer, an Austrian cantor and composer admired by Liszt,

*I am indebted in much of this discussion to Irene Heskes, *Passport to Jewish Music: Its History, Traditions and Culture* (Westport, Conn.: Greenwood Press, 1994).

Schumann, and Schubert, attempted to "purify" many of the traditional liturgical melodies that had been passed down through the Middle Ages. He sought to remove much of their ornamentation and trimmings to bring them closer in manner to the secular music of Europe, while at the same time preserving the soul of the ancient synagogue service and the general characteristics of cantorial music. The setting of the "Shema" that we all sing today is his, and the fact that we call cantors by that name is his doing as well. Until Sulzer, the person who led the singing in a synagogue service had been known as the "hazan" (as he still often is). But Sulzer had noted that Johann Sebastian Bach, the greatest of German liturgical composers, had held the position of cantor, or choirmaster, at Leipzig; and with no undue modesty, he set himself up as the Jewish equivalent.

Lewandowski, the choirmaster of the largest synagogue in Berlin, composed in the manner of Mendelssohn and published two very influential collections of his cantorial solos and choir responses for the full liturgical year. His music was known for its soulfulness, and I can still recall the feeling of sitting in synagogue and letting the sounds wash over me. As the historian of Jewish music A. Z. Idelsohn writes, "His greatest strength . . . is the cantabile, in the region between tune and recitative, in the free-flowing Jewish solo-singing, in minor. He created and developed a noble warm-breathing style of Jewish melody, purged of the tangled fungous growth of sentimentality." In 1871, Lewandowski published his *Kol Rinnah*—the first complete service for Sabbath and holy days, with detailed musical lines for the entire text of prayers. According to Idelsohn, "The singability and the freshness as well as the elaborate musical form of the choir parts, and last but not least the German *lied* style, made them so beloved by the Jewish congregations in Germany."*

I have a friend with a beautiful singing voice, and whenever we speak on the telephone, I ask him to sing some Lewandowski before hanging up. You might think this silly of me, but it's not, and he understands completely, and obliges. This was the music of my childhood, and to this day when I hear the music of the synagogue I can feel the touch of my father's hand on mine, can hear my grandmother's and mother's attempts to sing along.

Certainly, one reason the memories of those sounds are so potent is that they were snatched away so suddenly. On the Brahmsstrasse, as I've mentioned, my playmates were both Jewish and Christian, and if any of the latter stopped being my friend because of my religion, if ever I was the subject of anti-Semitic taunts, I have no memory of it. As a little girl, I was unaware of the currents of virulent anti-Semitism that were building to a crescendo in Germany all through my childhood, but they were there all the same. In the elections of 1932, when I was four years old, the Nazis were voted the largest party in the Reichstag. In 1933, Hitler was named chancellor, and the follow-

*A. Z. Idelsohn, *Jewish Music: In Its Historical Development* (1929; New York: Tudor, 1944), pp. 27, 282.

ing year he assumed the presidency. All I remember hearing about him was that he was a man who didn't like Jews.

How little he liked them, I didn't realize. In 1933 Jews were forced out of government service and universities and barred from entering professions. The Nuremberg laws of 1935 deprived Jews of virtually all civil rights. Many of the Nazi anti-Jewish laws directly related to music. In 1933, the government set up the Reich Culture Chamber to expel from the muscial world all individuals who did not possess the proper Aryan credentials. Slowly but inexorably, Jewish musicians were forced from the stage or recording studio and the work of composers even *suspected* of being Jewish was forbidden to be performed. Nazi musicologists were hard-pressed to explain how the works of figures such as Mendelssohn, Mahler, or Schoenberg–recognized internationally as part of the German musical tradition–could be tainted by "Judaic elements," but that did not prevent them from trying. By 1938 recordings by Jewish musicians and composers had been officially banned. There was an attempt to render concert halls, cabarets, and radio programs free of Jews. The popular singing group the Comedian Harmonists had been broken up because two of its members were Jewish; the opera singer Richard Tauber had left for London; the composers Kurt Weill, Arnold Schoenberg, and Wolfgang Erich Korngold had all fled to America. The list could go on and on.*

I knew none of this at the time of course; my parents, quite

*For a fuller discussion, see Erik Levi, *Music in the Third Reich* (New York: St. Martin's Press, 1994), pp. 39 ff., and Michael H. Kater, *The Twisted Muse: Musicians and Their Music in the Third Reich* (New York: Oxford University Press, 1997), pp. 75–129.

understandably, wished to spare me from the harsh truth. Interestingly, I do remember very well the folksong associated with the Hitler Youth, "Schwarzbraun ist die Haselnuß" ("Dark Brown Is the Hazelnut"). I have no idea where I first heard it, but I'm sure I had no awareness of its sinister implications. But any innocence and any illusions became impossible to sustain after Kristallnacht, on November 9, 1938, a night of mass violence against Jews. Many synagogues were burned, including mine. Classes stopped at my school. I didn't fully grasp the importance of these events, but I did have such a sense of anxiety that I slept in my parents' bed every night.

A week later, early in the morning, several large men–the SS–came to take my father away to a detention camp. A couple of weeks later came Chanukah, which had always been my favorite Jewish holiday–it's a holiday directed at children, and since I was an only child, I got a lot of attention! But it was very subdued without my father there to light the menorah and sing "Rock of Ages" as he always had. In his absence, I was the one who lit the candles.

About a month after that, I was separated from my mother and grandmother, too. In July of the preceding year, the Allied nations had met in the French city of Evian, and Switzerland, the Netherlands, Belgium, and France had each agreed to accept 300 Jewish children from Germany. Britain agreed to take 10,000–still, a small number considering Germany's total Jewish population of 550,000. I was one of a hundred children selected from Frankfurt to go to Switzerland, I still do not know how or why. And so, on January 5, 1939, my mother and grandmother put me on a train at the Frankfurt Hauptbahnhof. Some of the other children were a few years younger than I was, some a few years older. Most would never see their parents again.

I knew only one other little girl on the train, my friend Mathilde, and was otherwise surrounded by strangers. I was alone, but not alone in being racked by tears. Eventually, however, like children on a school outing, we began to sing, and I distinctly remember that it was I who started it all. Where else to begin but with the song of "Little Hans," who goes out to find adventure only to return home to his mother when she misses him too much? How else to continue but with "Kommt ein Vogel geflogen," with its prophetic words:

A bird comes flying to me,
Sits on my foot,
Has a note in its beak,
A greeting from my mother.
Dear bird, fly on.
Take my greetings with you and a kiss
Since I can't join you.
I must remain here.

CHAPTER TWO

Thoughts are free

The train ride was a long one, about ten hours, so we certainly went through all the songs we knew, exhausting our store of German, switching over to the Hebrew songs we had learned in school and synagogue, then back again. We crossed the Swiss border at Basel, where we were given cocoa and a snack, and I heard Swiss German for the first time. It sounded very different from the language of my childhood—very harsh, one might even say unmusical, to my young ears. Our ultimate destination was the village of Heiden, which is near Lake Constance, about fifty miles from Zurich. Fifty of us got off the train there and trooped through the town, a picture-postcard Swiss village. It was January 1939, and everything was covered with snow. I had never seen anything so beautiful in my life.

The place where we lived was Kinderheim Wartheim, a home for Swiss Jewish children who for some reason couldn't be with their parents. In some cases, the parents were divorced, in some cases they were traveling, in some cases they were dead. We German children slept at first in a barn that had been converted into an annex of the home. Before we came, it had been used only in the summer, when the home became a camp. The quarters were comfortable, certainly no worse than what I was accustomed to in Frankfurt. And the surroundings were spectacular. When we arrived, the four or five acres of grounds were deep in snow, but when spring and summer arrived the place really blossomed. There were lawns, lots of flowers, and a big vegetable garden with raspberries and strawberries. Next door was a farm, which reminded me of the one back in Germany that belonged to my mother's family and where I had often spent time during the summers. Here in Heiden I grew very fond of the neighbor's cows and of the sound of the cowbells and the way it would echo in the mountains.

But this was no alpine idyll. While we were living more or less comfortably and, above all, safely in Switzerland, our parents were back in Germany. Although at first we got letters from home, we had no idea of the precise nature of what was going on there. We knew it was frightening and grim, however.

Shortly after I left home, my father returned from the detention camp. He no longer had a business and was able to find work only as a gardener at the Jewish cemetery up the street from our apartment. By this point he realized fully that there was no future for Jews in Germany, and he went to the U.S. consulate to apply for permission to emigrate. All he received was a number: 49,280. Since the annual quota for emigration to the United States was less than 30,000, he knew this was useless. Still my parents held out hope of being able to leave the country, and in their letters to me, which I have to this day, they spoke about it all the time. In that, they had everything in common with the parents of all the German children at the home. The idea was that we would stay there for about six months and then be picked up by our parents or guardians to go on–to the United States, to Palestine, or somewhere else. This didn't happen by the time six months were over, so we went to the local police station to renew our permits. Six months later, we did so again. This went on for six more years, until the end of the war. The name of our residence, Wartheim–literally, "waiting home"– was more apt than we could have guessed.

To say that these were difficult circumstances for children and adolescents such as us would be a vast understatement, and it is remarkable how insensitively we were often treated at the home in Heiden. An experience on the first night set the tone. We all slept on the second story of the converted barn, and we discovered an opening in the floor for heat to come up from the wood-burning stove below. We looked through it, of course, and saw the people who were responsible for our care opening up our suitcases and examining their contents, making fun of our clothing for being unfashionable and worn-out. When they got to mine, they took for themselves the chocolate that my mother and grandmother had packed for me.

I don't recall any other instances of outright theft–after all, none of us had anything of value to steal–but in the more than six years we spent in Switzerland, we were, to put it bluntly, second-class citizens, and the attitude of the people supervising us was all too often consistent with the scene I witnessed on that first night. The worst of all was a woman named Fräulein Riesenfeld, who was herself a Jewish refugee from Germany.

She read all the letters we wrote to or received from our parents, and when one girl complained in a letter about some of the conditions, Fräulein Riesenfeld beat her in front of us all and forbade us from talking to her for days. I cannot imagine what motivated her to do something that was even more terrible, which was to tell us that we had been abandoned by our parents because they really didn't love us. I've since checked with others (not surprisingly, the group of us who went through this together have kept very close over the years), and they have the same memory. She said our parents were horrible people, like *Rabeneltern*, ravens who leave their young behind to fend for themselves. I knew this was not true, but of course, we never complained about her to our parents or to the people in Zurich who were responsible for the home. We knew that we were objects of charity and had better be quiet and thankful. The alternative to being there was much worse.

I have to say that despite all their shortcomings, the women who worked in the home provided us with some good things. One of these was classical music. I had never had any exposure to this before, and though our caretakers were terrible educators and not particularly humane, they came from cultivated backgrounds–they were mostly from Berlin–and felt some kind of an obligation to transmit their sense of culture to us. They read to us every Friday night, and they played symphonies, string quartets, and operettas on the radio and the gramophone. It was here, I am quite sure, that I first heard Mozart's *Eine kleine Nachtmusik*, still one of my very favorite pieces. And it was here, too, that I first sensed what it was really to *listen*. These German women were disciplined and wanted to make sure that we sat perfectly still and serious before the music, not treating what we heard as background noise. Of course, it was permissible for one of them, Frau Berendt, to sway and sing along with what was playing.

Incredible as it may seem, it was somehow decided that we, the German Jewish refugees, would act as servants for the Swiss children at the home. We went to school, but only for two hours a day. The rest of the time we did housework! We did the Swiss children's laundry, mended their clothes, and cleaned up after them. From the very start, I was given the charge of watching after some of the younger children, and this is the one task that I really loved and that made me feel good about myself. How proud I was to be entrusted with the care of the littler ones!

On a typical day I would be awakened at 6:15 in the morning to go over to the dining room with some of the other girls to straighten out the benches on which the children sat at breakfast. We would then go to the washrooms to comb their hair and to the dormitories to make their beds. After breakfast, I'd get a broom, a mop, and a pail of water from the kitchen and sweep the hallways and bathrooms, clean the toilets, and swab down the floors. When I was through, I'd go upstairs to do the bedrooms. This would take us up to lunch time. By mid-afternoon, we would be back at work again, sewing perhaps. In the evening, I would help bathe the children and after dinner would clean their shoes.

Every Monday was laundry day. We would wash the socks, underwear, and sheets of the other boys and girls in the home and would hang everything out to dry, even in winter, with frozen hands. Every Friday, before Shabbos, we refugee girls from Germany would put steel wool on our feet and slide over the wood parquet floor to clean it; then we would get down on our hands and knees to polish, until the floors were like mirrors.

And did we sing during these tasks? Not aloud, but I would hum constantly to myself, at first a tune I had made up for the jingle sung by Rumpelstiltskin as he danced about in solitude in the Grimms' tale. He was a little person, as I was, and also like me, his days were apparently filled with domestic chores: "Today I bake, tomorrow I brew" ("Heute back ich, morgen brau ich"). But where we were true soulmates, Rumpelstiltskin and I, was in our sense that it would be best to keep a part of ourselves hidden and thus safe from others in the midst of this drudgery: "Ah, how good it is that nobody knows / That my name is Rumpelstiltskin" ("Ach, wie gut ist daß niemand weiß / Das ich Rumpelstilzchen heiß"). Unlike me, of course, he had a plan for stealing the queen's baby, and probably not because he loved taking care of small children as I did. And I certainly wasn't one to have a tantrum and end up tearing myself in two as he did. But never mind; I hummed his song nonetheless.

Later, Rumpelstiltskin gave way to other songs, particularly the one I've mentioned earlier about the young girl who gets up before daybreak to kindle the fire. I now know that it is a setting by the nineteenth-century composer Hugo Wolf of a text by the poet Eduard Mörike. At the time, though, I just thought of it as the "Cinderella song," for who else would be tending the hearth so early in the morning? Cinderella and I were surely meant for better things than waking up before the crack of dawn to start the endless round of household tasks that were set for us: "This is how the day arrives, / I wish it would go away."

As I grew into adolescence, I became increasingly frustrated at not being allowed to go to a proper school. I knew I had a good mind, and I didn't want to spend my life peeling potatoes. A few of the boys were allowed to go on to the high school in the village, but the girls were not, and once I finished eighth grade my formal education was over. I hungered to study academic subjects and had by now gotten it in my head to become a teacher; instead, I was sent to the village once a week to learn how better to mend and iron and make beds. They were teaching me to be a maid! This helps explain why, ever since, I have absolutely hated housework (and if you saw my apartment, you would understand that I'm telling you the truth). And so I would hum my "Cinderella song," thinking sadly of our shared lot.

I still think of it as the "Cinderella song" even if there is a rather crucial detail that I seem to have passed over: Prince Charming has apparently toyed with the girl's emotions and flown the coop, for the song is titled "Das verlassene Mägdlein" ("The Abandoned Maiden"). The girl in the song is both doomed to housework *and* unlucky in love:

> Suddenly it comes to me,
> Faithless boy,
> That during the night,
> I dreamt of you.

Tear after tear
Runs down my cheek.

Certainly, when Walter, my first boyfriend at the home, broke up with me, I could *really* have wallowed in the melancholy of the song. But the day after he dropped me, I started up with Max, another one of the boys. Today, when I sing the song—as I often

do—it is especially when I am sad about being alone. Back then, it was about the housecleaning.

As I write about life at the children's home, I make it all sound very Dickensian. It wasn't, fully. For one thing, we had to stay in the barn only for a year; after that we were moved into the main house. For another, as I've said, the setting was extraordinarily beautiful. And most important, and what I can never lose sight of, being at Wartheim saved my life. Even the harsh regimen of housework has a reason behind it that is probably more poignant than cruel. There we were, an institution for Jewish children, many of us refugees, dropped into the picture-perfect tidiness of a Swiss village. Had the Christian inhabitants ever seen so many Jews before? Unlikely. Were they suspicious of our presence? I am sure. The people running the home must have felt under constant scrutiny. They had to demonstrate that as Jews we could be just as clean, just as orderly as the best of the Swiss.

For the home was a very Jewish environment. The food was strictly kosher (though we had meat only once a week), and we wouldn't turn on the lights on Shabbos. Music from the Jewish tradition provided significant sustenance, giving us the means to address the deeper issues that we could not bring ourselves to confront out in the open or even to think about. Certainly, this was true of our prayer. Every evening we said a prayer and afterward sang a song whose words went, "Here the guardian of Israel doesn't sleep and doesn't rest" ("Hine lo yanum v'lo yishan shomer Yisrael"). I was responsible for some of the younger children, as I've mentioned, and I remember singing the song with them every night as they went to sleep. It was always an emotional moment for me, because in Frankfurt my family and I used to sing the same song. But *was* God really watching over us? And if so, why was He not protecting our families as well? How could a vigilant God have allowed things to come to this pass? These are questions I now can raise, but ones to which I have no answer. Every Saturday evening, we all sang the "Shavua Tov" prayer with gusto, "Have a good week." This was also familiar to me from Frankfurt, and the tune gave me comfort, probably even more than the words. In some way, the melodies were a kind of replacement for our parents, in providing familiarity, warmth, and reassurance. In any case, they were certainly a help in preventing us from sliding into depression or despair.

At Wartheim we celebrated all the holidays that I knew from home: the High Holy Days, of course (Rosh Hashanah and Yom Kippur); Purim, with its carnival-like atmosphere and singing, always a favorite of children; Passover, melancholy to me in those days, for the seder was meant to be spent with one's family. I remember that one year I wrote a little play with music for Tu B'shevat, the holiday that celebrates the planting of trees.

And Chanukah, which I had loved so much in my early childhood in Frankfurt, remained important to me, maybe even more than ever before. Was it because now I truly understood that this was a holiday celebrating the triumph of light over darkness, of hope over adversity? Or was it because Chanukah had been the last holiday I had spent at home?

We would receive gifts during the eight days of Chanukah at Wartheim–in my case, always hand-me-down clothing because I was so small–and the glow of the menorah lights would fill me with pleasure and pride at being Jewish. But I made Chanukah last longer than anybody else. Above my bed, I had hung a picture that I must have torn out of a calendar. It showed a man holding a little girl in front of a lit menorah, and if I concentrated, I was sure I could actually see the candlelight flicker against their glowing faces. I was the little girl, I imagined, and the man was my father, even if unlike my father, he wore the full beard of a traditional Orthodox Jew. There was nobody else present. My mother and grandmother were excluded from this idealized family scene, to pay them back for the fact that my father had been missing from that last Chanukah in Frankfurt perhaps. They had not wanted to exclude him of course, I knew that; he had been forcibly taken away by the Nazi authorities. But my mother and grandmother had said that my father wouldn't be permitted to come back if I didn't leave Frankfurt and that it was he who wanted me to go to Switzerland. Looking at the picture over my bed, I knew this couldn't possibly be true. A father would never have urged such a thing. And looking at the picture, I would once again hear my father singing "Rock of Ages."

Thinking back on it now, after all these years, I hear him singing still.

I don't know what became of that picture. Probably, as I moved into adolescence, I found something that seemed more appropriate to my teenaged self for hanging over the bed. That picture is gone now, but the sense of sadness, remembrance, and catastrophic loss plays in my head.

Of all the comforts at Heiden, most important was that we children had one another. We realized that we needed to serve as each other's family and support, and we became very close. I still feel a strong bond with the other children from the Kindertransport and still frequently visit them in Europe and Israel. Just last month, when I was in Israel, I took ten alumni of the home out to lunch. This is more than sixty years after we arrived there! One special person was the Walter I've mentioned as my first boyfriend. Our relationship, which lasted from the time I was twelve until I was fifteen, was incredibly important to me. I was obviously lonely, and I felt that I wasn't in any way pretty or intelligent or desirable. Feeling that Walter loved me added immeasurably to my self-esteem and was probably crucial to my emotional development and my ability to form relationships in the children's home. I suspect that this friendship had an impact on my life that was greater than it would have been had I been growing up in a family. It also had an impact on my intellectual development, because Walter was very smart. He was one of the boys who was permitted to attend the local high school in the village, and he let me study from the books he carried home with him. At night, after we were supposed to be asleep, he would bring me his history, geography, and social studies texts, which I could work through (I couldn't make any sense of math or chemistry without the help of a teacher). Walter would hide in my bed while I crept out into the corridor to read by the hallway light, and when I was finished studying, I would go back to my bed, we'd kiss a little, and he'd go off, pre-

cious textbooks in hand. But for the purposes of *this* book, Walter is also important for another reason. He is the one who introduced me to the first American song I can remember, which I also think of as the first love song anybody ever sang to me: "You are my sunshine, / My only sunshine. / You make me happy, / When skies are gray." It's still one of my favorite songs.

As I think back on that time, it strikes me that we were always singing. In part I suppose this was because there were no toys to play with in Wartheim and we had to amuse ourselves in other ways; in part, certainly, we must instinctively have sung together as a way of strengthening our bonds. The music served many purposes for us, not the least of which was linguistic instruction. For example, we were not in any formal way taught Swiss German, which is quite different from the language we were used to from home–so we learned it through song. Unfortunately, there was a rather limited frame of reference in the lyrics. That is, I learned to talk about flowers in the mountains and not wanting to marry a farmer's boy, but not much else, it seems.

I am being facetious, but those are real songs. One I still remember and hum is "Es Burebüebli mag i nid" (the words go,

"I don't want a farmer's boy; I want someone who is more refined"). It's interesting that I would be singing that song because, as I've mentioned, my mother was a farmer's daughter, from the village of Wiesenfeld, some fifty or sixty miles from Frankfurt. (She had come to the city as a young woman to be a housekeeper in my father's family, they had had an affair, and she had gotten pregnant, after which she and my father got married. Yes, it's true–Dr. Ruth is a product of an out-of-wedlock, unplanned pregnancy.) Although I went to the farm in Wiesenfeld every summer to stay with my mother's family, the early experience of being brought up in the bourgeois society of Frankfurt am Main was decisive for me. Even if I didn't realize it, I was serious when I sang the words to that song: I *didn't* want a farmer's boy but someone of learning and culture. For the girl in the song, "It has to be a boy who is good-looking and special and nice." I'm afraid that there is no such guy in the picture, and she remains unmarried till her death. For me, things turned out quite differently, which may be why I can still sing "Es Burebüebli mag i nid" with a light heart whenever I'm with Swiss friends.

In those first few years at the home, until I finished the eighth grade and my schooling there stopped, my teacher was a Polish Jew named Ignatz Mandel. He wasn't the handsomest of fellows, and he walked with a limp–but he was as kind as Fräulein Riesenfeld was cruel. He had a difficult task in front of him, because he had to teach some forty students, ranging in age from six to fourteen, of all different levels of education and intelligence, all in one classroom and with few resources. Considering all that, he did a remarkable job, even giving us a smattering of English. And Ignatz was musically trained. He played the violin quite well, and he taught us quite a few songs. It frankly amazes me how many I remember.

I am a notorious pack rat, and I never know what I'll find when I investigate the various nooks and crannies of my apartment. The other day, I came across the *Schweizer Singbuch* (*Swiss Songbook*), a possession I had forgotten all about. When I first started thinking about this book, my friend Werner Gundersheimer remarked that it would be something like an archaeological dig. At the time I was a bit offended–I didn't like the idea of myself as being as old as ruins! But as I've proceeded, I've seen how apt his analogy is. I've had to dig and dig, and in the process have unearthed some remarkable and surprising things. The *Swiss Songbook*, excavated from under a pile of books in my living room, is a prime archaeological artifact, filled with significant clues.

It is a medium-sized book with a plain orange cloth binding, and on the front is the word *Primarschulstufe* ("Primary School"). Opening it up, you see that it is dated 1938 (the year before I arrived in Heiden). On one endpaper I find my original given name, "Karola," written by me in pencil; facing are the words (I am translating) "The book remains the property of the school and when you finish that school you are obliged to return it." But I didn't return it to the Swiss school authorities–rather amazing for a proper Jewish girl from Frankfurt such as me. Not only that, but the book is one of the few possessions I have carried with me through life, from Heiden, to a kibbutz in Palestine, to a student residence in Jerusalem, to a walk-up flat in Paris, and then on to the United States. It is in remarkably good condition considering its travels, so it must have meant quite a bit to me. And now I open it again, at the age of seventy-five.

Looking at the songs in the book, again and again I experience the shock of recognition. On the last page is a poem by Marie von Ebner-Eschenbach, entitled "Ein kleines Lied" ("A Little Song"), that asks, "How is it that one little song is so beloved? . . . It contains a little sound, / A little harmony and melody, / And an entire soul." A bit sentimental, perhaps, but as I leaf through the volume, the memories come flooding back. I find myself in some of the songs and am once again a child and adolescent in Heiden; I look at others and can't but wonder at the distance between the things of which they sang and the realities of my existence.

We sang songs of comfort and optimism, as if the very act of singing could set our world aright. "Hab oft im Kreise der Lieben," began one (with words by the Romantic poet Adalbert von Chamisso):

Often, surrounded by loved ones,
I have rested peacefully on the fragrant grass,
And sung a little song to myself,
And everything was right and good

I have also been lonely and troubled,
In an anxious and gloomy mood,

And then I sang once again,
And everything was once again good.

And some of the things I've experienced,
I've stewed over in quiet rage,
Then I started once again singing,
And everything was once again good.

You should not continually complain to us, then,
Of everything that causes you pain,
Just cheerfully, cheerfully sing,
And everything will once again be good.

Did I find consolation in the memories of a loving family that this song evoked and in its assurance that any troubles one might have would easily pass? Most definitely. I'm quite sure that the song's lesson of optimism found in me a most willing pupil. "A *Jecke* (German Jew) doesn't cry," I always say, and when life deals me a blow, large or small, "in typical Ruth Westheimer fashion" (I also say), I simply move forward. But our problems in those days were not ones that could be solved with a song, and if this one helped me through difficult times, I nevertheless think how poignant it is that we could believe in its words.

"Wer nur den lieben Gott läßt walten" was another song we often sang, this one found in the section of the book titled "In Praise of God":

Whoever trusts in God to do as He will,
And trusts in Him always,

Will be wonderfully sustained
In all times of need and sorrow.
Whoever trusts in God, the highest of all beings,
Has not built on sand.

The Swiss song compilation is not a Jewish book, of course, and this was one of the few hymns that could serve for us as well as for Christian children. Indeed, the message it conveyed—that if we trusted in God, everything would turn out all right—was precisely what my grandmother wrote to me in each letter she sent. This was comforting to a child, but how wrong it turned out to be, and how tragic if it was somehow religious faith that taught anyone to stand passively by as the horrors of the Holocaust mounted.

"Freut euch des Lebens," "Rejoice in Your Life," counseled us to take pleasure in all things while the lamp still burned and the rose still bloomed—a classic carpe diem song—as if the world around us was all flowers and glowing lights. According to the words of the "Beresina-Lied" ("The Beresina Song"), another one of our hopeful standbys, we went through life like travelers in the night; if the lyrics promised that daylight would come and our sorrows would be lifted, at least they acknowledged that for now we were surrounded by darkness. This was a song that spoke to me then, and speaks to me still, and on a number of levels. Its positive message is one I am able to embrace, yet it recognizes that life is an uncertain journey. I could hope for the morning filled with sunshine that the song promised, but I was also coming to feel like the wandering Jew, a person with no homeland to call her own and no place that would accept her.

"We all sit so cozily together, / And love one another so much. / We brighten one another's lives so, / Oh, may it ever remain thus." These are the words to the song of camaraderie that jumps out at me from the pages of the *Swiss Songbook*. Sing it gaily and *gemütlich*, read the instructions at the top of the page, and this we surely did as a group. Here was a song that celebrated my ties of affection and shared experience to the people who were now my only family, the other children at the home. But the name of this song is "Wechsel der Dinge," "Changing Things," and these family members, too, would disappear, like the ones before: "It cannot remain so forever, / Here under the changeable moon. . . . / Who knows, then, how soon we'll be scattered / By Fate to the East and the West?" We'll meet again as friends some day, the song cheerfully assures, but how could I be certain? My experience so far had taught me that I would lose the people about whom I most cared, so it was safer not to get too attached to anyone. Is it any wonder that I should have felt this way? And that I would continue to feel this for a very, very long time? Indeed, it was not until the birth of my first child, Miriam, many years later, and my marriage to Fred that I learned to think differently.

One section of the *Swiss Songbook* is titled "Nature" and is filled with songs about strolling through the woods, listening to the birdies singing, walking in fields of flowers, climbing in the Alps. I am certain that my love of the outdoors was nourished by all those sweet and memorable songs. Even more songs are collected under the heading "Wandern," or "Hiking," and in the Swiss context, this makes perfect sense.

Our main form of recreation in Heiden was hiking, in fact. The home had very little money and couldn't afford to buy equipment for sports or any other activities. So we hiked–not mountain climbing but long walks through the hills. And we were provided with good shoes (never new for me, because I was so small and could always wear what the others had outgrown). Besides the exercise, being outdoors in the fresh air, seeing the flowers in the fields, was very good for my spirits.

Of course, while we hiked, we sang; in German such songs are called *Wanderlieder*, and I still remember many of them. Two songs we hiked to were "Das Wandern ist des Müllers Lust" ("Wandering Is the Miller's Joy")–not in the famous setting by Franz Schubert but in another version, by Karl Zöllner–and "Wem Gott will rechte Gunst erweisen." This latter is from a poem by the great Romantic writer Josef von Eichendorff, and it has a beautiful setting by Schumann, but again, it was a different version we learned from our schoolbook. "When God wishes to show his true favor to someone," we sang, "He sends him out into the wide world, / And points out His miracles / In mountain and wood and river and field." The author Alfred Häsler, with whom I worked on my first book, *The Story of Karola Siegel*, used to say, "You can only experience a landscape when you take a stroll, a hike through it," and I firmly believe that. Walking is essential for me–outside, inside the house (even when I am on the phone), wherever. It helps me get my thoughts in order and feel that I am occupying my place in the world.

But what place was I occupying back then? We were constantly singing about the splendors of the forests, flowers, and mountains. If I were still in Frankfurt, this would have seemed pure poetry perhaps, but here in Heiden, the beauties of nature were all around, and real, and an inseparable part of our everyday existence. And this nature was inextricably a part, too, of the songs that made up the largest section of my purloined *Swiss Songbook*, the ones dedicated to *Heimat.*

Heimat is a notoriously difficult word to translate into English, for it means not simply "home," but also "native place" and "mother country." In the *Swiss Songbook*, the *Heimatlieder* were the patriotic songs, and it was a patriotism expressed through praise of the landscape. I suppose this is not so different from the way in which a song like "America, the Beautiful" functions, but in the Swiss context it was difficult to know where a song about hiking through the mountains left off and hymn in praise of country began:

> I love you, my homeland,
> On account of your beauty.
> It greets me from every rock face,
> And needs no artful cultivation.
> The wreath of mountains, the lakes, the valley,
> They call aloud, and all together:
> There is but one Switzerland.

Every August 1, on Swiss independence day, we would go to the village for a celebration; there was a big bonfire, and the men would hold huge, billowing flags and swing them about as sport. We couldn't eat the food because it wasn't kosher, but we could sing the songs, and we did so with great gusto. One, I remember, talked about the country as a white cross in a field of red, and we knew exactly how to understand the image, for from our position of safety we could see Germany, right across Lake Constance from where we stood (later in the war, we could actually see the Allies bombarding Friedrichshafen, on the opposite shore). Only once did we feel that there was a real possibility of Switzerland's being invaded—on May 10, 1940, when Hitler invaded Holland. I remember that we thought we would have to go into the mountains to hide, that I had to prepare a knapsack with food and hang it on my bed when I went to sleep. In general throughout the war, there was a constant state of readiness, but we felt as safe as possible under the circumstances.

Looking back, the whole situation was in equal parts ironic and heartbreaking. I sang the songs in praise of Switzerland with great enthusiasm, for as I've said, I knew that I had been spared from internment—and likely death, as I came to realize—only because the Swiss had taken me in. Singing the patriotic songs was in some way an expression of gratitude. Moreover, the tunes were very catchy and rhythmic, and it was easy to get swept away by them. From the time I was a little girl in Frankfurt, playing musical circle games with my friends on the street or letting the familiar sounds of the synagogue wash over me, music had always been about being a part of a larger group entity. Now, here in Switzerland, I needed so urgently to *belong*, and although it was an impossibility, I wanted so desperately to have a *Heimat* to replace the one I had lost. But at the same time, I knew deep down that Switzerland was not really mine. It has occurred to me only recently how sad it was that I should have been singing these patriotic songs every day–about the mountains and lakes and how much love there is–knowing that I really wasn't a part of any of it. For the Swiss made it quite clear that when the war was over, we would not be encouraged–or perhaps even permitted–to stay. What other conclusions were we to draw from the way we were treated? Our guardians wouldn't say it outright, but they would shake their heads and ask, "Where are we going to send you?" The meaning was clear. But I couldn't really admit it to myself–I think the sense of hopelessness and loneliness would have been too much to bear.

Certainly, dark moods crept in around the edges. The message of the music I loved wasn't all positive and upbeat. Of course, being an adolescent–and a true romantic–I sometimes gave in to despair. One turbulent song I remember from the schoolbook is "Der gute Kamerad" ("The Good Comrade"), a dramatic and haunting piece about two soldiers, one of whom is killed by a bullet that comes flying toward both of them and is remembered by his surviving friend. Another song I used to sing over and over to myself is "Ein Jüngling liebt ein Mädchen" ("A Young Man Loves a Maiden"). The text is by the nineteenth-century writer Heinrich Heine, the music by Robert Schumann, and it tells a rather contorted story of a boy who falls in love with a girl, only to see the girl fall in love with another man, who in turn loves and marries someone else, which provokes the first girl to marry yet another person out of spite–leaving the poor first young man out in the cold. As Heine's lyrics note, "It is an old story, / But it stays forever new. / And for those to whom it happens, / It breaks their heart in two!" Was this really an everyday occurrence in the outside world? The thought was not reassuring.* Another song with words by Heine, and beautiful music by Felix Mendelssohn, was much more comforting to my adolescent being, and I sang it quite a lot. It is called "Leise zieht durch mein Gemüt," and its words go,

> Sweet chimes
> Are softly filling my soul.
> Ring, little springtime song,
> Ring far and wide.
> Go forward, . . .
> And when you see a rose,
> Tell her that I greet her.

This was more like it.

The most important song for me during those years was "Die

*I recently came across a book by Marcel Reich-Ranicki called *Ein Jüngling liebt ein Mädchen* (Frankfurt am Main: Insel Verlag, 2001), about Heine's and other German songs. In discussing *Ein Jüngling*, he makes an interesting critique of the music by Robert Schumann: "He didn't designate the tempo, so it's always sung with gusto. But it should be alarming and somber. We don't hear the despair of the loves. Schumann missed the hidden drama between the lines." Of course, maybe if the melody were somber, it would all be too much to take. Incidentally, Reich-Ranicki has a fascinating history. He was born to a Jewish family in Poland and as a boy emigrated to Berlin, where he developed a lifelong fascination with German culture. He escaped the Nazis during the war, including two years spent hiding in the cellar of Polish peasants. After the war, he lived in Poland but returned to Germany in 1958, and since then he has been one of the country's major writers and cultural commentators.

Gedanken sind frei" ("The Thoughts Are Free"). I must have sung it to myself a million times when things were difficult, for of all the songs I learned in Heiden, this nineteenth-century melody is the one that gave me greatest sustenance:

Thoughts are free,
Who can guess them?
They fly past us,
Like nighttime shadows.
No man can know them,
No prison contain them;
It remains ever thus,
Thoughts are free. . . .
And let someone close me
Into a dark dungeon,
I will mock my torment
And the actions of men;
Then my thoughts
Will tear open the prison gratings,
And split the walls in two:
Thoughts are free.*

I was older now but still taking some of the same consolation I had from Rumpelstiltskin years before: nobody could know

*The words are found in *Des Knaben Wunderhorn*, a collection of folk poems published between 1805 and 1808 by the great Romantic writers Achim von Arnim and Clemens von Brentano. There is a setting by Gustav Mahler, which is not the version I know from Switzerland.

who I really was or what I really felt. Any feelings of despair or hopelessness were mine and mine alone—but I could also think and dream of anything at all, I could aspire to the world if I wished, and nobody in Kinderheim Wartheim could mock me, for nobody need know. I had a sense of power over my own interior life, and that gave me tremendous consolation.

As I have mentioned before, all of the German songs that refuse to leave my head and heart present complications. On the one hand, they are meaningful to me because they represent the culture from which I come and they connect me to some of my earliest memories and formative experiences; on the other hand, they will forever be associated with the people who exterminated my family and destroyed the life I had known. It is a contradiction I will never resolve, but I know that Beethoven, Bach, and Schubert were not Nazis and that Nazi guilt does not hang upon them. I love much of this music and it will always be a part of me. And it is only now that I realize just how much of classical and Romantic German culture I absorbed through the songs I learned, with their words by Goethe, Heine, Eichendorff, Chamisso, or music by Mozart, Schumann, and Mendelssohn.

But there were other sounds in the air as well. I've mentioned that my first American song was "You Are My Sunshine." My next was "On the Good Ship Lollipop," though I didn't know the words then and still don't. I had only the smallest smattering of English, learned from Ignatz Mandel, but we were shown quite a few British and American movies—*Mrs. Miniver, How Green*

Was My Valley, *Waterloo Bridge*, *Gone with the Wind*. The ones that made the biggest impression on me were the Shirley Temple films. She was the idol of my early adolescence, and I thought only in paradise—or maybe America—did people look like her, with her curls and dimples and crinoline dresses. She was so spirited and alive and made others happy, and I loved that. She was like a princess, surrounded by wealth and beauty, even if she was short like me and seemed to be an orphan, too. Perhaps there was hope for me as well.

Near the end of the war, a group of American soldiers who had been prisoners somewhere spent time in a camp near Heiden. Some of the older children from the home went to visit them, and the Americans taught them some more English songs, which they in turn taught the rest of us: "My Darling Clementine," "My Bonnie Lies over the Ocean," and "It's a Long Way to Tipperary." Another song we must have learned from the Americans was "Lili Marleen," and perhaps no other popular song of World War II had so curious a history. Its composer, Norbert Schultze, had written it to be recorded by the German singer Lale Andersen in 1939. The Germans started using it on nightly radio broadcasts to the troops, and British soldiers heard it and started singing the song, in garbled German or in one improvised English version or another (some of them apparently a bit risqué). Soon the song, which told of a soldier pining for his faithful love, was properly translated into English and recorded—and became a bona fide hit on both sides of the conflict. So there I was in Switzerland, singing a Nazi song, in its beloved English version, as taught to us by the Americans.

Another song in English—after a fashion—that I remember is "Auld Lang Syne." I don't recall who taught it to us and can't imagine what they thought they were up to, but I do remember that we used to sing it often, standing in a circle holding hands with our arms crossed, trying our best to make some sense of Robert Burns's Scots text. What on earth did I understand of lyrics like "And surely, ye'll be your pint stowp! / And surely I'll be mine! / And we'll tak a cup o' kindness yet, / For auld lang syne"? Surely, they were baffling to a group of Jewish children from Germany, waiting out the war in Switzerland. (I have just now consulted the Robert Burns website, by the way, and have finally found out that "be" means "pay for," a "pint-stowp" is a tankard, and "auld lang syne," literally means "the old long ago.") But somehow we understood the feeling of the song. Because of my early experiences, I am always afraid that a person whom I love will disappear. Though a *Jecke* doesn't cry, my eyes tear up when, at a railroad station, I see people I don't even know saying good-bye to each other. So the nostalgic sentimentality of "Auld Lang Syne" affected me deeply.

I remember quite a few lullabies from Switzerland. But now, as someone given responsibility for the younger children, I was the singer, not the one sung to. There was "Bona nox" ("Good Night"), a playful round in four voices—and five languages—with words and music by Mozart. I can only imagine how I mangled that one! At the other end of the spectrum was the haunting and beautiful "Schlaflied für Mirjam" ("A Lullaby for Miriam"), with words by the Austrian Jewish poet Richard Beer-

Hofmann, and music by Carl Orff. We were taught this by Herr Bernsohn, a very learned man who briefly was director of the home:

> Sleep, my child, sleep, it is late.
> See how the sun goes to its rest.
> Behind the mountains, it dies in redness.
> You, you know nothing of the sun and of death.
> Turn your eyes toward the light and the sunshine,
> Sleep, so many suns will be yours.
> Sleep, my child, my child, fall asleep. . . .
>
> Do you sleep, Miriam, Miriam, my child?
> We are but the river bank, and deep in us runs
> The blood of those who have come before, and of
>   those who are to come,
> The blood of our Fathers, uneasy and proud.
> They are all inside of us, who can feel alone?
> You are their life, and their life is yours.
> Miriam, my life, my child, fall asleep.

Beer-Hofmann wrote this lyric in 1893, on the birth of his daughter, Miriam. This was long before the rise of the Nazis and Beer-Hofmann's own wartime emigration to Switzerland and then America, but the poem seems colored both by its sense of the turbulence of Jewish history and by an awareness of the death and darkness that still lay ahead. I have remembered this song my whole life but never sang it after Switzerland, not even to my own daughter Miriam, for if I found solace in the song's assurance that we carry within us all who have come before and all who are still to come, I could find no easy comfort for my child or myself in the knowledge that we carry, too, all their disquiet. This is, for me, a lullaby in name only and full of foreboding for the Jewish people.

As I have already indicated, among the many difficult things about our time in Switzerland was our uncertainty about the future. We never even considered the possibility that Germany would win the war—that was too horrible to contemplate—but what would become of us after an Allied victory, and where were we to go? The Swiss would not keep us, and we had no families to which to return. After my first couple of years in Heiden, toward the end of 1941, the letters from my parents stopped coming. In time I learned that they had been deported to Lodz, where, as in other Polish cities, Jewish ghettos had been created. I now know that in all likelihood, they were killed at Auschwitz, where most of the Jews from the Lodz ghetto were shipped, but the knowledge that my parents had probably been exterminated seeped into my consciousness only slowly. With the end of the war, lists began to come out from the death camps and ghettos of those people who had survived, and these were read to us in the children's home as soon as they became available. We all held our breath, waiting for the sound of a familiar name, but the right names never came. It was only many years later, when the lists not of those who lived but of those who had perished were made available, that I found some record of my father, grandmother, and maternal grandparents. After each name is the single word *died.* I found my mother's name on a list with the word *verschollen*, disappeared, next to the name.

There is a song that I learned during my later years at Heiden that expresses much of the sense of hopelessness and displacement I was feeling as the war wore on and finally ended. I don't recall exactly who taught it to me, though it was perhaps Ignatz Mandel, nor have I ever been able to determine its source, though I felt sure I was headed in the right direction a few times during the writing of this book. I do know that I did not make up the song myself, for my dear friend Ilse, who was with me in the home and whom I've mentioned before, remembers it as clearly as I do. And I know that over the years, I must have sung this song to myself at least a million times. "Jeder Mensch auf der Welt / Hat sein eigenes Land," it begins:

> Every person in the world
> Has his own country,
> And there he is at home.
> Only one people in the world
> Has no homeland of their own,
> And every day there stands before them
> The eternal Jewish question,
> "Whither, Jew?
> Who in the world will take you?
> Where can you be safe?
> Where do you need not be worried
> About your next day?
> The world is so large,

And for you it is small.
A door is still open,
But for you it is closed.
There is no place in the world.
You are a Jew."

The sentiments expressed here are unique in Jewish song, and I have found two other pieces that are in some ways strikingly similar to mine, though both are in Yiddish. "Yiddisher Vanderer," or "Jewish Wanderer," was written by the Russian-born composer, lyricist, and playwright Abraham Goldfaden sometime before 1908. It is a lament for the enforced homelessness of the Jewish people in this world and contains both the lines "A Yid bistu" ("You are a Jew") and "Nishtu keyn plats far dir" ("There is no place for you"). Goldfaden composed it for his operetta, *Dr. Almasada, or the Jews of Palermo*, but the song took on a life of its own. It apparently had special meaning for turn-of-the-century Jewish immigrants to America, who used an English translation of it to learn the language of their new homeland; and Bob Freedman, curator of the wonderful archive of Yiddish music at the University of Pennsylvania that bears his and his wife Molly's name, remembers that his mother-in-law knew this as a song sung in Bessarabia in 1919 in response to the pogroms in Ukraine. Even closer in many ways is "Vu Ahin Zol Ikh Geyn?" ("Where Shall I Go?"), a song with music attributed to Osar Strock and words written by S. Korntayer, a Yiddish actor who perished in the Warsaw ghetto.

The Jew is hounded and plagued,
Every day is unsure for him. . . .
He has no hope, no safe place.
Where shall I go,
Who can help me?
Where shall I go
When every door is closed?

The lament was sung in ghettos throughout eastern Europe during the war and in displaced persons' camps after the war's end. It seemed to sum up in so many ways the sorrows of the Holocaust and the hopes of Zionism. But it, too, is not my song. The melody that I know is different from both of these others, and of course the words that Ilse and I remember are not in Yiddish, a language neither of us knew then, but German. Perhaps Ignatz, who was originally from Poland, had himself translated some Yiddish original for us. I may never know. What I do know is that the hopelessness I felt was so deep, I could admit it only in song.

Only one people in the world
Has no homeland of their own,
And every day there stands before them
The eternal Jewish question,
"Whither, Jew?"

The war finally ended, and going back to Germany was unthinkable. In order to go to another western European country, you had to have a relative already there, and I didn't. And the United States to me was like a Shirley Temple dream–glamorous, enticing, and absolutely out of the realm of possibility.

I had gone with one of the adults from Wartheim to be interviewed for admission to a kindergarten teacher training program. Before the day of interview, I studied the contents of the Swiss children's songbook, not so I could sing them–because I knew by then I didn't have a voice–but because I somehow thought the songs would prove how much I belonged here. I don't recall that my new knowledge came up, but never mind; I was accepted to the school.

It is clear that when I look back on Switzerland, it is always with the knowledge that we were not welcome there and with the assumption that I could never have stayed. But perhaps the door was not as firmly shut as I usually think. The school had guaranteed my tuition and even offered to provide me with pocket money. If I had enrolled, I probably would have found a way to remain in the country. I would have married a Swiss man and would today be a fat little retired schoolteacher, still named Karola, speaking Swiss German by now, if never quite thinking Swiss thoughts. Certainly, I would never have become Dr. Ruth, but who could even have imagined that possibility back then? I would have had the promise of a stable life of a sort I had not known since leaving Frankfurt.

So, why didn't I enroll in the school?

Something in my gut told me not to. I knew in my heart by then that the life in Frankfurt was lost forever, and I felt the sorrow of having so little that could tangibly tie me to it. Six years before, I had carried my favorite doll away with me but had given it to another little girl on the train that brought us to Switzerland to cheer her up. I still had a washcloth from home with my initials printed on it (other children at Wartheim had had more expensive, embroidered ones) and a few cherished family photographs. I regretted that there was not more, not even a prayer book from my parents. But the melodies I'd heard every week in synagogue and sung on Shabbos anchored me strongly to the memory of my father, mother, and grandmother and somehow kept them alive for me. I saw that I would have been the only Jew in the teacher training program, and I think now that it was the deep hold of the synagogue music that helped me realize that I would need to be in a Jewish environment to thrive. I would stay with most of the children–now teenagers–with whom I had been for the past six years, and would go with them to an uncertain future in a country about which I knew practically nothing. I had my answer to the "eternal Jewish question." I would go to Palestine.

CHAPTER THREE

Our hope is not lost

The women and men who ran Kinderheim Wartheim were not Zionists, but they were realists and must have assumed that when the war was over, most of us would be going to Palestine, then a British protectorate. So they were receptive to visits from a number of representatives of a group called Youth Aliyah, which was dedicated to encouraging young people to emigrate. The Hebrew word *aliyah* means "up," and that is the way going to Israel always was—and still is—referred to. (This is literal as well as symbolic: the road from the Israeli airport to Jerusalem is uphill, and even now many people, myself included, get out of the car before they arrive at the city and climb the last few hundred meters on foot. The first stop in the city for me and many others is the Western Wall, where I slip between the wall's stones a piece of paper hoping for peace and good health.) The organization had been founded in 1933 by Recha Freier, the wife of the chief rabbi of Berlin, to help resettle young people who had been disenfranchised by the anti-Semitic laws of the Nazis. I had never heard of it when I was in Germany, which was not surprising given my age and my parents, who were not Zionists.

But it was very effective. Directed from Palestine by Henrietta Szold, the extraordinary American-born woman who had headed the Jewish Publication Society and been one of the founders of Hadassah, Youth Aliyah set up elaborate networks to secure visas, transportation, housing, and education to enable some five thousand German teenagers to come to Palestine before World War II. Youth Aliyah gave them agricultural training to prepare them for life on the kibbutzim, and taught them at newly established Youth Aliyah boarding schools. After the war, the organization, which was allied with the women's group Hadassah in the United States, would succeed in bringing an additional fifteen thousand young people to the country from all over Europe, most of them Holocaust survivors or, like me, orphans of the Holocaust. Today Youth Aliyah villages continue to play a vital role in the absorption of young newcomers, as well as offering thousands of disadvantaged Israeli youths a second chance.

The Youth Aliyah representatives' message must have struck a responsive chord in me, for as early as 1940 I wrote a letter mentioning Theodor Herzl, the founder of Zionism, and the next year I noted in my diary that we had a "celebration" for him. In September 1942 I wrote an essay fantasizing about what would happen "After the War." In it I described arriving in Palestine: "My grandparents on my mother's side and my grandmother on my father's side are staying with relatives in Tel Aviv. My parents and I and an uncle who has been here for two years are going to a neighboring kibbutz. Mama and her brothers and sisters are getting used to farmwork again. Papa, too, has found a pleasant job, and I will teach in the kindergarten of the children's house of the kibbutz. We have a little house all to ourselves."

It would be three years before the war really ended, of course, and during that time the children's home was a hotbed of Zionist proselytizing. The Youth Aliyah representatives were expert at instilling enthusiasm and knew exactly how to appeal to adolescents who were both idealistic and emotionally needy. It didn't hurt, of course, that most of the organizers were good-looking young men. There was one in particular on whom I had a crush. His name was Avram, and he was originally from Belgium. I could overlook the fact that he had a humpback because he seemed brilliant to me and had dark, piercing eyes–and the most beautiful singing voice. In adolescent confusion, I confided in my diary, "Now I want to be very honest. Is it only his personality or the entire philosophy of the organization that was attractive to me, or is it because I'm attracted to anything new?"

A time-honored way of infusing people with zeal is through music, and we were taught many Zionist songs and dances. Instead of the plaintive lament about the Jew's homelessness that I knew, Avram and the others taught us songs that joyfully assured us of our place in the world. "Whither, Jew?" There was a homeland waiting to be ours, they promised, ready to welcome us and build us up as fine young men and women. The hope and the music were intoxicating.

All these songs were in modern Hebrew, and this was our introduction to that form of the language. When we finally did get to Palestine, we could speak only haltingly, but we were able to sing and dance with the established settlers and our fellow recent arrivals. Of course, the songs are still vivid in my mind. "Artzah Alinu," a catchy and upbeat melody, almost a march, welcomed us to the land: there is work to be done, but we all shall benefit.

> We have immigrated to the Land of Israel, we have
> immigrated to the Land of Israel.
> We have already plowed and have also sown,
> But we have not yet reaped.

"Vetehezenah Eynenu" ("Look to You Again, Jerusalem") has music by Nisan Cohen-Melamed and lyrics filled with hope for a homecoming after long wandering: "And may we live to see when You return to Zion with mercy." "Ki Mitziyon" ("From Zion's Crest"), by Emanual Amiran, has a rhythm that makes you want to leap up and dance, and lyrics based on a Scripture verse: "From Jerusalem, from Zion's crest, / Shall go forth the law by which man is blest."

With my childhood love of songs in which the singers act out roles, it was a sure thing I would respond to "Usheavtem Mayim" ("And You Shall Draw Water"), whose music is by Shlomo Hoffman, with a Hebrew text based on Isaiah 12:3. As we sang, we danced the horah, and once again, as in some of my earliest memories of Frankfurt, I could join in a circle combining music and play. We would take a few steps into the center, then move to the right and the left, as if we were drawing water from the ground:

And you shall, with joy, draw water
From the springs of salvation....
Oh water with joy....
Water, water with joy.

Here in these songs was my fantasy of Palestine as a land of milk and honey, where the water was sweet and plentiful and the land was fertile. What I found when I arrived was completely different, but that is getting ahead of myself. In Switzerland, I sang the Hebrew melodies with my loudest voice and copied the lyrics that were most meaningful to me into my diary.

A majority of the fifty refugee children at Heiden went to Palestine, with the rest going to other countries where they had relatives. Our group left Wartheim on July 7, 1945, a month before the war in the Pacific was over. We first took a train to the Swiss town of Bex, where we spent two months preparing for our great move. We then traveled to Marseilles, from where we were to set sail. This was a long train ride, and to pass the time there was music. I remember, in particular, singing "Ki Mitziyon," and I remember, too, that just like six and a half years before, it was I who led the group in song. But now we were not crying.

At Marseilles, tents had been set up for us on the beach. We stayed there for two nights, then took a train to Toulon, where we boarded a ship bound for Palestine. It was very crowded—there were six hundred of us on board—and I slept on the deck with many of the others. It was early September, and the weather was mild, and the stars overhead were brighter than any I had ever seen. Our journey lasted six days, and it seems to me that we must have sung and danced to the Zionist songs without stop. But our excitement was dashed when we arrived in Haifa. We had to wait in a camp, called Atlit, while the British sorted out our papers. After having seen pictures of Jews being held in German concentration camps, it quite naturally upset us to be incarcerated in Eretz Yisrael, in the Land of Israel.

Fortunately, after a few days, I was allowed to leave. Along with about thirty-five other new immigrants, I set out in a convoy of covered trucks for the kibbutz, or collective farm, that was to be our new home. It was called Ayanot, near the small town of Nahalal, not far from Haifa, and upon arrival I experienced another shock. The people who ran the kibbutz were Polish Jews in the main and they had an understandable distaste for all things German. Some of that cruelly extended to us. They immediately demanded that we discard our Teutonic-sounding first names and adopt new ones more in keeping with the new land. And so I was no longer to be Karola but Ruth. I did keep "Karola" as a middle name, though, hoping against hope that my parents were still alive, and thinking that if they saw a reference to "Ruth K. Siegel," they would somehow know it was me. Even today, for professional and official purposes, I give my name as Ruth K. Westheimer.

Like most of the kibbutzim, Ayanot was primarily agricultural, producing olives, oranges, apples, grapes, grapefruit, and tomatoes. There were cows there, too, and though the landscape and climate were completely different, the whole place pleasantly reminded me of my grandparents' farm in Wiesenfeld, where I had spent every summer as a little girl. But life on the kibbutz was very hard–in most physical ways and even in some emotional regards, harder than life in Heiden. We slept four to a tent, and though this may sound romantic, it wasn't, especially in the rain. And on what kind of mattresses did we sleep? On ones made of straw, just like those used by the feckless Tyroleans who had lost everything in the song my grandmother and I used to hear sung by peddlers in our Frankfurt courtyard. Let me tell you, a feather bed is better.

There was enough to eat, but many things were in short supply–milk, for example, which we had only once a week. Even the oranges, for which the country was famous, weren't very good; the best ones had to be set aside for export. In keeping with the communal philosophy of the kibbutz movement, neither money nor personal possessions were permitted. We were all given just two outfits–a white shirt and a pair of pants for Saturdays, and a shirt and a pair of shorts to wear while working during the week. And work we did. At first I picked tomatoes and olives in the fields and felt that I was, indeed, helping to build up the land. But then I was switched to housework. I worked two hours in the kitchen, two hours doing household chores, two hours cleaning toilets, and so on, until I completed my eight hours of work a day. Was it for this I had come to Palestine, to be a maid after all? The songs from Germany and Switzerland had not left me, and as I cleaned, I sang some of the more desolate ones to myself. At the end of the day, however, we would all gather together to sing "Ba-ah M'nuchah" ("Rest Has Come") to mark the transition from the work day to some well-deserved evening tranquility. The song was written by David Sambursky:

Rest has come to the weary
And tranquility to the laborer,
A pale night stretches out
On the fields of the Jezreel Valley.
Dew below and moon above,
From Beth-Alpha to Nahalal.

How is this night different from other nights,
There is silence in Jezreel,
Sleep, valley, land of beauty
We are your watchmen.

Hard work was only one of the many and uncanny similarities between Heiden and Ayanot. On the kibbutz, as in Switzerland, our group was considered second-class citizens. As I have said, the old-timers, most of whom were Polish Jews, resented us, in part, no doubt, because the German Jews—not untouched by snobbism, I have to admit—had always looked down on *them.* In addition, I can imagine that the very sound of the German we spoke among ourselves was hateful to their ears. We had little choice, for in addition to making us work especially hard—and making a seventeen-year-old girl clean toilets all day long is really not acceptable–they didn't bother to teach us Hebrew. As at Heiden, the main thing that helped us learn the new language was all the singing we did. And here is another similarity to Heiden: we had only ourselves to depend on and turn to, and singing and dancing was the glue that helped us stick together.

For Jews in Palestine in those years, this was no coincidence. The settlers who hoped to shape a nation had decided early on that one important way to build up a sense of solidarity was through music. As a nation of immigrants, Eretz Yisrael lacked a long-standing tradition of folk songs such as I had sung in Switzerland and Germany, words and melodies that had been handed down from generation to generation. Even the language of the land, Hebrew, was being revived after centuries during which it had been used only in prayer, never in day-to-day communication. So a whole generation of composers and lyricists sat down and *wrote* a body of brand-new Hebrew "folk songs," about work, the homeland, the soil, the landscapes of Galilee, and the countryside. Natan Shahar has consulted various anthologies and collections of songs (*shironim* in Hebrew) published up to 1949 and has come up with a master list of 4,073 songs, an astonishing three quarters of which were written by a core group of just thirty-two composers.* Many of these were known as "shirei Sochnut," or "Jewish Agency songs," after the umbrella group that helped people come to Israel. All the Agency songs contain

*See his "The Eretz Israeli Song and the Jewish National Fund," *Studies in Contemporary Jewry* 9 (1993): 78–91.

the hope—so strong you can almost touch it—that a Jewish state will be created. We had been taught many of those songs in Switzerland, as I've mentioned—"Artzah Alinu," "Ki Mitziyon," "Usheavtem," and others. Now, on the kibbutz, they were the soundtrack to my life.

People who were around in those days still like to sing the old songs. In fact, just a few nights ago I went to a celebration of the anniversary of the creation of the State of Israel, and afterwards I went to a nightclub where a performer was singing many of them. It was a wonderful evening, because usually when I say to an Israeli, "I want you to sing those Jewish Agency songs," the person just smiles at my nostalgia. Today they are considered irredeemably old-fashioned. For me back then—for all of us—they were tremendously alive. Their themes were no different from those of many of the songs I had sung in Switzerland. Once again, it was all about patriotism and my love of the land, but with a crucial difference. In Switzerland, I always had the sense of playacting as I voiced the words. However loud I would sing, the songs weren't really for or about me. Now I believed in them with every ounce of my being.

As important as the singing was the dancing. Folk dancing had always been a big part of the lives of the Jews who had come to Palestine, because such activities engender enthusiasm and a sense of collectivism. Participating in a group festivity, no one needs to be an expert dancer or a trained singer. Everybody joins, singing the same melody and dancing the same steps. In 1944, an official folk-dance movement was launched. It culminated in a large-scale festival at Dahlia in the Ephraim Mountains in 1947. Five hundred dancers participated, and 20,000 spectators attended—a huge number, especially considering the size of the overall Jewish population.

The performers at that festival took dancing to the level of art. At my kibbutz—and at every other kibbutz in the country—folk dancing wasn't a matter of art but of just about everything else: recreation, socializing, exercise, expression of national, communal, and cultural values. And I loved it. I feared by now that I was such a terrible singer that my voice might set an entire group sing off kilter, but dancing I could do. Every Friday after work, we would dance the night away. We would never dance a waltz or any other couple dance; that would be too bourgeois (though I do remember with pleasure that once we bent the rules to do the Krakovia, a Polish partner dance that dates back at least to the early nineteenth century). Mostly it was the horah. That dance is now familiar to everyone from weddings and bar mitzvahs, or at least from *movies* of weddings and bar mitzvahs, but when we were taught it by the Youth Aliyah organizers in Switzerland, it was a new thing to us. One of many European circular chain dances surviving from ancient times, the horah had its recent origins in Romania. Once it was transplanted to Israel/Palestine, it lost its association with special occasions and became the dance to be done whenever a group of people wanted to have a good time. It also gained a technical refinement: the circle rotates as everyone does "grapevine," or crossover, steps. Even so, it is so simple that anyone, even the most rhythmically challenged, can do it, and do it well. Another advantage was that it provided an extremely cheap form of entertainment. All you needed was a room and one person with an accordion, sometimes just a harmonica. And believe me, any guy (it was always guys) who could play one of those instruments was a big hero.

The Friday night dances not only forged a sense of solidarity within a kibbutz. They also helped foster relations between kib-

butzim. Either we would go to another kibbutz on Friday night, or we would be the host. I can still see the trucks that were used as transportation (there were no cars or vans), their cargo beds crammed with the benches on which we sat. Once the dancing began, it didn't stop for hours. I loved the rhythm and the melodies and the twirling around, until I was almost in a trance, almost able to forget my troubles–the loss of all I had once loved, the everyday drudgery, the fact that I was a stranger in a strange land, where they spoke a language I could not properly understand. So I would dance until the wee hours, would get a few hours of sleep, and then start cleaning toilets again. So much for Saturday as the day of rest! This much I know: if someone could find a way to bottle the energy of youth, they'd make more money than Bill Gates and Rupert Murdoch combined.

The fact that the dances were held on Friday night itself indicates how different was the setting in which I now found myself. Such an activity would have been a cause for scandal in Frankfurt or Heiden. The kibbutz, however, was not very religious, much less Orthodox. This was the first time in my life I had lived in such a secular environment. On Friday evenings, there was no prayer before bread or after a meal. The only thing we would do was sing "Shabbat Hamalkah" ("Sabbath Queen"), a solemn but joyous prayer with music by Yoel Valbe and lyrics by S. Bass : "Approach, approach, blessed one, / Sabbath Day, Day of Rest, / Come upon us, the Queen of Sabbath." And then we would go to dance.

We never went to synagogue, and though we observed the Jewish holidays, it was more in a secular than in a religious sense. Passover, for example, was primarily about the return of spring rather than the biblical exodus. Already, less than two weeks after our arrival in Palestine, I wrote in my diary, "Today was Yom Kippur. I fasted, not out of conviction but for the sake of my parents, because I know they would be unhappy if I would deny so radically everything that has to do with religion." From a background steeped in religion and thoughts of God, I had come into an environment where God did not really seem to exist. This mind-set was reflected in the music. I had been steeped in the prayers of the synagogue that my father had sung, which were all about God and His power. Now we sang songs about building a country or working in the field. The point was clear–God was fine as far as He went, but when it came to tilling the earth and building houses, He was not much help at all.

I left Ayanot after a year. I still wanted to be a kindergarten teacher, and I had heard of another kibbutz with a seminary that trained people for the occupation. The only problem was that the course cost money and I had none. But I devised a plan whereby I would work in the kitchen for a year at a time, in return for which I could take the course in alternate years tuition free. Before the first year of kitchen work was over, however, something better–glorious, really–came up. I was in contact with a woman named Liesel Engel, a distant cousin of my mother's who had emigrated to Jerusalem before the war. Through her I met a lovely couple by the name of Goldberg, and now Mrs. Goldberg had helped me to get a place–and a scholarship–at a kindergarten seminary in Jerusalem!

I moved to the city immediately, and just as immediately fell in love with it. For one thing, Jerusalem *was* a city, and it offered up unimaginable excitement and opportunities to a young woman who had been stuck for the past eight years among the trees, mountains, and fields. Jerusalem, too, was unique among the cities of Palestine for being of mixed population: there were Jews, Arabs, and Christians, all of whom viewed the city as a holy and sacred place. Driving uphill to the city, seeing the beautiful golden sunset on the "Jerusalem stone" of the buildings, I felt a deep sense of history and continuity; at Passover, Jews the world over wish for "next year in Jerusalem," and here I was. And, at the age of eighteen, I had my own room for the first time in my life, in a young women's residence. Very soon I was very busy, with my studies, with part-time jobs as a waitress, babysitter, and maid–and with boyfriends. There was no longer time or opportunity for the communal singing and dancing I had experienced at Ayanot. Still, in Palestine in those days, the strains of folk music were frequently in the air, and whenever people got together, there was a good chance they would end up dancing.

Liesel, my mother's relation, was a woman of education and refinement, and once a week I would go over to her apartment for a sandwich and conversation. Here was a *Jecke*'s refuge! Since coming to Palestine, I had met people who had practically tried to shame me out of my Germanness, but Liesel held fast to all she found that was good in the culture in which she had lived for much of her life. In many ways, her flat could have been in Frankfurt or Berlin, not the least because she and her late husband had brought hundreds of recordings with them from Germany. These took up an entire wall of the apartment, and here, before my eyes, was more classical music than I ever knew existed. No visit was complete without our listening to at least one of the records on the gramophone. Mozart was a favorite–I already loved *Eine kleine Nachtmusik* from Heiden–and the Romantic *Lieder*, too. Beethoven's Ninth Symphony was a revelation. Liesel was much kinder than Fräulein Riesenfeld back in Heiden, but in one respect the two were alike: it was made clear to me from the start that when the music was playing, I was to keep my mouth shut or I would not be invited back. These were difficult conditions for someone as talkative as I, but I didn't want to run the risk of being cast out. Only after the music ended was I allowed to ask questions, invariably about the composer and his love life. Never mind; after my experience on the kibbutz, where the older inhabitants from eastern Europe had no use for anything German at all, it was wonderful to be able to hear those composers and see how their music could still be respected and loved. Here, in the bourgeois comfort of Liesel's living room, was a whole new world, and though it would shock my comrades from the kibbutz if they ever found out, I keenly felt its appeal. I dreamed of having such a space of my own, perhaps even some day a salon, where musicians, writers, and people of culture could come to meet, as I'd heard they did in nineteenth-century Berlin.

I started at the seminary in April 1947, and that November, the United Nations adopted a plan whereby the British would leave Palestine and the country would be divided into a Jewish state, an Arab state, and a small internationally divided state surrounding Jerusalem. This, unfortunately, led to a period of guerrilla warfare between the Jews and Arabs. Idealist and joiner that I am, I decided to enlist in the Haganah, the Jewish underground army, while still continuing my kindergarten-teacher studies. After completing my basic training (including learning how to take apart and put back together a machine gun with my eyes closed), I was frequently a messenger or a guard, standing on a rooftop and watching over a barricade where the Israeli soldiers stopped each car to check it at the entrance to the city.

The following May, following the U.N. plan, the British high commissioner for Palestine left the country, and David Ben-Gurion proclaimed the independence of the State of Israel. The whole country erupted in celebration. A bunch of us piled into a truck and drove through the city, where we saw people singing and dancing on every corner. What they were singing most of all was "Hatikvah" ("The Hope"), the Zionist anthem that would now be the anthem of a new nation.

The song has an interesting history. Its text was written by an itinerant Galician poet and staunch Zionist, Naphtali Herz Imber, in the late nineteenth century. The words are these:

In the Jewish heart
A Jewish spirit still sings,
And the eyes look east
Toward Zion.

Our hope is not lost,
Our hope of two thousand years,
To be a free nation in our land,
In the land of Zion and Jerusalem.

There were several attempts to set these words to music early on, but the version that stuck was by Samuel Cohen, a Moldavian immigrant living in Palestine in the 1880s. Cohen matched Imber's text to a melodic line found in the beautiful symphonic poem *Vlatava* (*The Moldau*) by Bedrich Smetana, which is itself based on an eastern European folk melody; there is some difference of opinion as to Cohen's direct source here. In 1905, the song was unofficially adopted as the anthem of the international Zionist movement, when it was sung by all the delegates present at the Seventh Zionist Congress. It was taken up by Jewish partisans in Europe during World War II, and during the pre-state era in Palestine, it was often played in the underground movement as a kind of rallying cry.

In recent years, some people in Israel have advocated replacing "Hatikvah" with a new anthem. They point out that the lyrics were written by a nonnative Hebrew speaker and sound awkward and archaic to modern ears; and whether it was based directly on the work of a Czech composer or an old folksong, the melody, they note, doesn't even have Jewish origins. Others object that the tune is in a minor key and that it sounds plaintive rather than joyful, or that it has a distinctly eastern European cast, thus excluding the traditions of the more than half of

Israel's Jewish citizens who come from Sephardic traditions or Arabic lands. I see the critics' point, but I would not replace "Hatikvah" for the world. I thrill as the music swells on the word "hope"–*hatikvah*–and was moved almost to tears this autumn by a concert performance of the song in which each singer on stage came forward in turn to sing that one key word in a different language.

More than half a century has passed, and the hope and idealism of those early days has been replaced with something far less giddy and more complicated. But hearing the strains of the song still take me back to the beginning, to that truck ride through the city, to the sense that the whole world was ahead of us and anything was possible.

Alas, the celebration didn't last long. The day after independence was declared, the armies of Lebanon, Syria, Jordan, Egypt, and Iraq invaded Israel, and all of us in the military were back on active duty. On June 4–my twentieth birthday–I did my regular tour of surveillance and, about noon, came home to the youth hostel where I was living. As soon as I walked in the door, I heard the sirens scream, the signal that we were to go immediately to the shelter in the basement. I said to myself, "I don't want to be bored sitting there with nothing to do," so I ran upstairs to my room to get a book. This was a big mistake. I was back in the lobby on my way to the shelter when there was a tremendous explosion. An Arab bomb had detonated right outside the building, sending shrapnel everywhere.

People started screaming. Plaster was flying all around me, and dust came down from the ceiling. A girl standing right next to me fell to the ground. I found out later that she was killed, along with another girl and a soldier. As for me, all of a sudden I found myself sitting against a wall, with a searing pain in both legs. Hannelore, a girl from Heiden who also lived in the hostel, was trying to unlace my new shoes, which I had just gotten for my birthday. I looked down at my feet and saw they were covered with blood. "Do I have to die?" I asked.

Thanks to the work of the doctors at the Hadassah hospital, I did not. They removed shrapnel from all over my body, including one piece in my neck and many in my feet. I had multiple abrasions just above both ankles, and the top of one foot was all gone.

After the doctors performed their magic, I convalesced in the basement of the hospital, which at one time had been a library. There were no beds left, but I was so small that I could fit on a bookshelf, and that's where they put me. One thing that helped my morale was that I was the only woman in a room full of men—including a handsome, blond male nurse from Romania with whom I was infatuated. I pretended I couldn't eat by myself so that he would feed me. A truce was declared on June 11, a week after I was injured, and after that he would pick me up from the shelf, take me in his arms, and carry me outside, where he'd set me down under a tree in the sunshine. During the lull in the fighting, I went to Haifa to recuperate. I stayed with friends, and every day, a man named Shaul, who had been my boyfriend at Ayanot, came to visit me from a small town nearby. He would sing to me and always the same Hebrew song, "You Wait for Me and I'll Return," which I think of as the second love song ever sung to me. When I was better, Shaul and my other friends begged me not to go back to Jersualem, but I said that my obligation was there, and I went. Shaul stayed behind and that was the end of our relationship. Apparently, I wasn't too broken up about it, because shortly after I got back, the male nurse from the hospital got in touch with me, and we had a short, happy love affair.

Israel won the war, of course, and final armistice agreements were reached in January 1949. That spring I finished my studies and got a job as a kindergarten teacher. My students were the children of Yemenites, who had recently been flown to Israel to escape persecution in their native country. It was a fascinating introduction to a culture that was completely unfamiliar and exotic to me. For example, the Yemenite men had two wives, one younger and one older; they would get an apartment with one room and a terrace, so that one wife was always out on the terrace and one was inside. After a while, they switched. I sometimes felt that it was my job to bring not only the children but also their parents from the ancient to the modern world.

Not long after that, I left Israel. Though I didn't know it at the time, I would never return there to live. I have visited regularly through the years, though, and in recent times, since I have been able to afford it, I have gone back at least once a year. The music I hear now on the streets, on radio, in hotels and restaurants sounds like generic pop with Hebrew words, not at all the patriotic and melancholy melodies of the early years. The old songs are brought out only for remembrance days. The dancing has, if anything, changed even more. It's all disco style, with no touching. The horah, along with the communal feeling it symbolized, is gone. The changes make me a little wistful, but I don't spend a lot of time or energy bemoaning them. The way we sang and danced was right for us then; the way the young people today sing and dance is no doubt right for them now. To expect everything to remain frozen and unchanged is a notion too romantic and foolish even for me.

But when someone starts singing the old songs, I do love it.

CHAPTER FOUR

Je ne regrette rien

The reason for my leaving Israel was a serious relationship that came along about the same time as my job teaching kindergarten. Through friends, I met a man named David. At the time he was a soldier, stationed near Jerusalem, but he wanted to be a doctor. Once we started dating, we and some friends, Miriam and Nachum, would go dancing every Friday night. We'd go to a coffee house—there were not many of them open in Jerusalem in those days—where recorded music would be playing. And we weren't doing the folk dances of the kibbutz, but waltzes and tangos—the steps that my fellow kibbutzniks would have deemed outrageously bourgeois. I loved it so much that I refused to let the bits of shrapnel that were still in my legs slow me down.

I liked David very much and was flattered by his interest in me. After only a few months of courtship, he proposed marriage. I immediately said yes. Ever since losing my mother, father, and grandparents, I had felt alone and adrift in the world, and David had a big and loving family that I could automatically join if I became his wife. Perhaps you can already sense what was wrong with this picture. I did not. In November 1950, we were married, on the terrace of my relative Liesel's apartment in Jerusalem.

By this time, David had been discharged from the army. There was no medical school in Israel back then, so he–we–had to go abroad. The logical place for him to study was Europe, and where in Europe could be better for a young couple than Paris? I had left France by boat as a refugee just a few years before. Now

I was returning a married woman, taking the first plane ride of my life. I arrived in Paris and found a place to live not too far from the Sorbonne, the University of Paris. We were in a working-class neighborhood, and we couldn't afford anything fancy, of course–just an unheated furnished room on the third floor of a walk-up, with cold water in the flat and a bathroom two flights down. I got a job as a kindergarten teacher for a Jewish agency and eventually was able to take an additional job, teaching Hebrew to French Jewish children. But first I had two obstacles to overcome. For starters, none of the children understood German and Hebrew, the only languages I could speak. So I took a crash course in French and Yiddish and was able to learn them quickly (I seem to have a facility with languages). My second problem was one I already noted–I cannot carry a tune, or I felt I could not carry a tune, which amounts to the same thing and is a serious impediment for a kindergarten teacher. I have already described how the ladies at the nursery school had me take singing lessons with an elderly gentleman, to little effect. At that point, I solved the problem by singing softly and letting the kids lead the way.

It helped, I think, that however softly I sang, the kids could pick up on my enthusiasm for the French songs. They tended to have catchy tunes and rhythms and memorable words; the sheer repetition of them helped me better learn the language and develop an accent that I have been told is quite respectable. And I still sing these songs–to myself–to this day. One of the really popular ones with the kindergarteners was "Meunier, tu dors," a musical attempt to wake up a lazy windmill keeper. We sang the song slowly at first, and then, as it got faster and faster, we all swung our arms around to imitate the movements of the windmill. It was so much fun that I never understood why "Meunier, tu dors" didn't catch on in the United States. Another wake-up song that most definitely did travel was "Frère Jacques," the sixteenth-century rhythmic round. I seem to remember it from a much earlier stage in my life–from Switzerland, probably, where it was called "Bruder Jakov," and perhaps even from Germany–and we sang it in my Israeli kindergarten, too. These were all Jewish milieus, but there was never any objection to addressing ourselves in song to the lazy monk, Jacques, who had to get up early in the morning to ring the church bell.

Nor was there any problem with singing "La petite église" ("The Little Church"), written by Charles Fallot and Paul Delmet in 1902. Odd as it seems, even at that time I had an affinity for churches. It had all started in Switzerland. Sometimes when I was very sad and lonely, I would to go to a tiny church in the mountains near the children's home, with just my diary for companionship. I loved the way the silence was broken by the church bells inside and the cowbells outside. Part of the allure, no doubt, was that it I thought of it as a forbidden place. Today, I love churches still. Not long ago, I visited the Mormon Cultural Center in Jerusalem for an organ recital. The music was spectacular and the view of the holy city out the window fabulous, and I remember thinking, "If only the people of the many faiths who worship here in Jerusalem could come together like these heavenly notes."

I have never been one to feel excluded from the festivities at Christmastime, and Christmas in Paris was something else! I had seen Christmas being celebrated in Germany and in Switzerland, of course, and as I've mentioned, I loved many of the carols. But I was in a protected Jewish environment in both places, and this was the first time I really understood how important the holiday is to Christians–and of course, the French did it up with such style! We certainly didn't sing "Silent Night" in the kindergarten, but I heard it elsewhere, and it had a strong pull on me, I'm sure because it was a song I remembered from my childhood in Frankfurt. A more secular Christmas song I loved was "Petit Papa Noël" ("Little Father Christmas"), which was and is hugely popular in France. Someone who brings gifts to all the little children of the world, even the orphans–I thought that was a fabulous concept! How could I not be drawn to a father figure who would provide me with love and care? You may find this odd, but I had something of the same feeling on my first trip to Italy, when I stood in front of Michelangelo's statue of Moses. And it wasn't just the beard. More than anything else, what I felt was the loss of all a father could have shown me, told me, and offered me if only he had not been taken away so many years before.

But I was not dwelling on the negative, if I can judge by the songs I recall from Paris. "Tout va très bien, Madame La Marquise" ("Everything's Fine, Madame Marquise") was a favorite. This was a music-hall-style song that originally became popular when it was adopted by strikers in 1936. It's a wonderfully droll piece in which a butler tells a marquise over the telephone that everything's all right at home–except that her gray mare has died in a fire. How did this happen? she asks another servant to whom she places the next call. It was when the stables burned down, but everything's fine. And how did the stables burn? she asks another. They caught fire when the château burned down, but everything's fine. But how did the château catch fire? The marquis knocked over the candles when he committed suicide upon learning that he was ruined. But everything is otherwise fine: "Tout va très bien." And that was Ruth Westheimer's refrain. Our small group of Israelis had no money for wine, which in France is akin to having no air to breathe. I used to tell people to pretend that our water was wine, and they would make affectionate fun by calling me "Madame Marquise," clueless about the disaster. I would laugh and respond with one of my favorites of the new songs I'd learned, "Demain il fera beau sur la grande route." The French have been in the vanguard of many things, and here, they were years ahead of Little Orphan Annie:

Tomorrow, it will be fine on the great road . . .
Tomorrow is a new day,
Tomorrow all the birds
Will sing along the way,
Tomorrow.
If today heavy clouds
Darken the sky to gray,
Tomorrow, it will be fine on the great road.

This is a traditional song that I've sung to spur myself on thousands of times over the decades, though I can't say for sure where I first heard it. We certainly didn't have a record player or radio, but music seemed to be in the Parisian air (have I seen too many movies?). Once in a while we did manage to scrape together enough francs to go to a neighborhood music hall to hear singers whose names have been forgotten by me and, I would imagine, by history as well. We also sometimes went to the Comédie-Française and the Théâtre du Châtelet, where we sat in the very last row, which was called the *poulailler*, or "chicken coop." I remember the first time we went to the theater. When I saw how much fabric—yards and yards of it—had been lavished on curtains and costumes, I actually got upset. I had been used to wartime, orphanage, nation-building austerity and to wearing the same clothes for years, and I literally couldn't comprehend the extravagance before my eyes. (I had a similar reaction to seeing the rows and rows of steaks and roasts in the butcher shop windows.) I eventually got over this and became a real theater fan and a champion autograph hound. After performances, I would wait outside the stage door, where an assistant would gather everyone's autograph book, bring them in to the star to sign, and return with the goods.

In Paris, I once again had to make peace with patriotic songs that were not meant for me. I could enjoy the pride and sense of belonging that they expressed, but I realized at the same time that these feelings were not my own. I certainly heard "La Marseillaise," but it did not make much of an impression on me at the time. I would grow tremendously sad, however, listening to "Ma Normandie," a song written in 1835 by Frédéric Bérat. The opening lyrics are,

> When everything is reborn in hope,
> And winter flees far from us,
> Under the beautiful sky of our France
> When the sun comes back more softly
> When nature is turned green again
> When the swallow has returned
> It is then that I love to see my Normandy once again.
> It is the land that gave me the day.

Now, I had no associations with Normandy whatsoever. I had certainly never been there. But "Ma Normandie" had such an impact on me because it reminded me that I would never sing such a song about the place where I was born. In future years, I would return to Germany, something I could not easily imagine back then in Paris. But I was correct in intuiting that I would never do so with a feeling of nostalgia or with the hope that I would someday live there again. This song, and others like it, underscored for me the fact that almost everybody feels a strong connection to the place from which they come. I do not. Perhaps it would be different if there were a cemetery for me to visit, with the graves of my parents and grandparents. But there is not, and even though I now come to Frankfurt at least once a year and have good friends there, I confess to feeling no particular connection to the place. I know this intellectually, but it is never really brought home emotionally until I hear a song like "Ma Normandie."

There is, as you have realized by now, a flip side to my optimism and joie de vivre. It's not despair but a vein of melancholy that I have always tapped into through music more than anything else. Of course, the French are famous for their bittersweet songs, mostly about lost or unrequited or unhappy love affairs of some kind or other, and these found an extremely receptive audience in me. Perhaps the poignancy of accounts of loving and not being loved back resonated with me because of my life history; the melancholy of the songs gave a voice to the sadness and insecurity I had often felt. But wonder of wonders, if the songs were melancholy enough, I could let them do their sad work—and be more upbeat myself.

(However much I like the passion of the French chansons, by the way, I confess that I never really cared for the Portuguese fado that my husband Fred introduced me to years later. Fred, too, was born in Germany—in 1927—but his parents had moved to Portugal in 1938. Fred had been sent for safety to America in 1941, to live with an uncle down South. His parents stayed put, and they still lived in Portugal when he and I met. Fred loved the fado and tried to pass his enthusiasm on to me, but I always found it *too* pessimistic. The Portuguese seem to sing directly and achingly from the wounded heart and to invite their listeners to share and wallow in their depression. I hope that's not my style. Call me silly, but I had a similarly negative reaction to "Tit-Willow," the Gilbert and Sullivan song from *The Mikado*, about a bird who kills himself because of "blighted affection": "He sobbed and he sighed, and a gurgle he gave, / Then he plunged himself into the billowy wave." My friend Al Kaplan used to sing it all the time when we were hanging out together a lot in New York in the late 1950s. Admittedly, with my lack of command of the subtleties of English, I probably took it all too seriously, and the wry humor of the song escaped me. Still, I was and am baffled and somewhat offended by the idea of a bird committing suicide for love.)

Getting back to the bittersweet French love songs, one of my favorites is a traditional one, "Là-haut sur la montagne." "On top of the mountain," a man sings, "I heard crying. / Ah! It is the voice of my companion and I went to console her." "Ah! If I cry and if I sigh," she tells him, "It is out of regret for having loved." As I've said more than once, I hardly ever cry myself, and the same had always gone for sighing—I saw it as a sign of giving in to sadness, and while singing about sighing in a song like this made it sound very romantic, I didn't approve of it in real life. In fact, I used to criticize a friend of mine, Bill Kunreuther, for sighing too much! But then I read in a journal that sighing is a sign of mental health, and I had to apologize to him and tell him he should sigh as much as he wants.

"Plaisir d'amour" ("The Joy of Love"), with words written by

Jean-Pierre Claris de Florian and music by Jean-Paul Martini, is probably one of the loveliest French songs of all time and seems as fresh and delicate today as it must have been when it was composed two centuries ago. The singer tells of having given up everything for his lover, Sophie, who promised she would remain true as long as the water flows into the stream. The water still runs, but she has left him for someone else. What can he do but sing? The refrain, "The joy of love is but a moment long, / The pain of love lasts a whole lifetime," certainly spoke to my romantic, twenty-three-year-old German Jewish soul.

But what was I to make of the cheerfully amoral "J'ai deux amants" ("I Have Two Lovers"), a song made famous by the singer and actress Yvonne Printemps? Here she sang as a kept woman, who explains how much better it is to have two men than one:

> I make each one believe
> That the other is the serious man.
> My God, how stupid men are.
> They each give me the same amount of money
> Exactly each month,
> And I make each believe
> That the other gave me twice as much.

Before coming to Paris, I had never been in a place where women were so very open about their sexual powers. Certainly I had never seen prostitutes before, and here they were, brazenly offering their wares all over the city. I was simultaneously scandalized and intrigued. In time, I came to fancy myself quite the libertine, offended not so much by the sexual frankness surrounding me as by conventional morality. And I found a song like "J'ai deux amants" naughtily appealing!

It had, in fact, astounded me at first just how full of sexuality many French songs were—and this included some of the ones I sang with my kindergarten students! Every child in France—and probably every child studying French anywhere in the world, for that matter—knows "Au clair de la lune" ("By the Light of the Moon") or at least its first stanza or two. You probably remember how it begins:

> "By the light of the moon,
> My friend Pierrot,
> Lend me your pen,
> To write down a word.
> My candle is dead,
> I have no more light,
> Open your door,
> For the love of God."

Pierrot, however, is already in bed and responds that he has no pen anyway; his friend should knock at the neighbor's door, where there is a light. This may be as far as you had to memorize, but French school children know what happens next, when the friend follows Pierrot's advice:

> By the light of the moon,
> The amiable fool

Knocked at the brunette's.
She responds quickly,
"Who is knocking at the door?"
He says in turn,
"Open your door
For a god of love."

Which she does. What would *you* do, after all, if the god of love came knocking? "I don't know what they found," the singer notes tactfully, but in the darkness, the door closes behind them.

Even more risqué is the early eighteenth-century "Auprès de ma blonde" ("Next to My Blonde"). This one was originally a drinking song, and its refrain simply and emphatically repeats how good, how good, how good it is to sleep next to the blonde of the title. I don't remember for sure if we sang this one in kindergarten, though I know it is a song schoolchildren sing. In any event, I liked the spirit of it long before I was a sex therapist. Looking back, I really do believe that I developed much of my "liberated" attitude toward sexuality from the French people and their music. In any case, I loved that jaunty song, and whenever I meet French people today, I can't help but sing a few choruses to them.

The reigning king and queen of the French chanson when we were in Paris were Edith Piaf and Marcel Mouloudji. Piaf, "The Little Sparrow," is the more famous of the two worldwide. Born Edith Giovanna Gassion in 1915, she spent much of her childhood in a bordello run by her grandmother, performed with her father, a circus acrobat, and became a singer on the streets of Paris at the age of fifteen. By her early twenties, she was a star. Her life—which ended in 1963 after years of unhappy relationships, alcoholism, declining health, and dependence on painkillers—was tumultuous, and audiences responded as much to her tragedies and passions as to her incredibly expressive voice. We never had a chance to see Piaf in person, but I knew and enjoyed her music, especially "La vie en rose," that lush love song which has become so closely identified with Paris that it has unfortunately become a cliché ("When he takes me in his arms, / He speaks to me softly, / And I see life as rose colored"). Piaf didn't record another of her signature pieces, "Non, je ne regrette rien," until 1960, some years after I had left Paris, but I have to confess, of all her songs, this is the one that is most meaningful to me. Defiantly marching on, a victorious combattant in life's emotional battles, she sings,

> No, I regret nothing!
> Neither the good that's been done me
> Nor the ill;
> It's all the same to me! . . .
> No, I regret nothing!
> It's paid for,
> Swept away,
> Forgotten.

As far as my own actions are concerned, I have tried to lead my life according to this principle. Certainly, all kinds of things might have turned out differently if I myself had acted differently, but to sit around and brood about this accomplishes nothing. Better to learn, if possible, and then move on to the next challenge. After any setback, I pick myself up, emphatically utter one word—"Done!"—and try to move on.

I identified with Piaf because she was tiny like me, but I loved Mouloudji (as he was simply known) even more. He was born in Paris in 1922, the son of an Algerian father and French mother, and like Piaf, had a hardscrabble childhood on the streets. He trained as a mime with the celebrated actor Jean-Louis Barrault, and shortly before World War II he was adopted as a sort of mascot by the Left Bank intellectuals like Jean-Paul Sartre, Robert Desnos, and Jacques Prévert. He had an extraordinary career. He became a prize-winning novelist, and after the Liberation he blossomed as a composer and singer. I confess, I was attracted to his deep dark eyes as much as to his songs—and the combination was lethal! He had many hits, but my favorite was the deeply passionate "Comme un petit coquelicot" ("Like a Little Poppy Flower"), with words by Raymond Asso and music by Claude Valéry. This was a huge success in 1951, and it won for Mouloudji the first of his two Grands Prix du Disque. The singer recounts how he met a girl in the countryside and kissed her with such ardor that he left a mark on her breast like a poppy. But there is another man, whom she does not love, and when the singer returns the following day, he finds his lover lying still and half naked in the field, once more with a mark like a poppy on the exposed white breast above her heart, but this time formed by three drops of blood. Wow!

After his death in 1994, Mouloudji was buried in the Père Lachaise cemetery. On a recent trip to Paris, I made a pilgrimage there and had someone take my picture next to his grave. I couldn't help noticing that there were a lot of pilgrims to another grave, people much younger than I and dressed in a somewhat less conventional fashion, shall we say. I asked, and it turned out they were paying their respects to Jim Morrison. I confessed to my friend that I didn't know who that was, and he explained to me that Morrison, the lead singer of the Doors, was a musical icon to a later generation. I stuck by Mouloudji.

I did not visit the grave of Yves Montand, who is also buried in Père Lachaise, but that was perhaps unfair of me. Certainly, during the years I lived in Paris, he, too, played loudly on the soundtrack of my life. I think especially of his recording of "Les feuilles mortes," made in 1947, just a few years before my arrival, and still one of the most popular records ever in France. The Hungarian-born composer Joseph Kosma had set the words of Jacques Prévert to music, and these are very different from the schmaltzy and rather simple lyrics of the song's English version, "The Autumn Leaves." In English, you may recall, the days grow long, I'll hear winter's song, but I miss you when the leaves start to fall. In the French, it is infinitely more complex and melancholy, as the separation of lovers seems to be a part of nature's grand scheme:

> The dead leaves are gathered in a shovel,
> The memories and regrets, as well,
> And the north wind carries them away
> Into the cold night of forgetting. . . .

Life separates those who love one another
Softly, without making any noise,
And on the sand, the sea erases
The footprints of parted lovers.

Looking back on this period now, I know there was a significant reason why I was responding to all these unhappy songs about love gone wrong: my own love life had gotten rather entangled. After our initial excitement at living in Paris together, David and I had grown apart. I think we both had come to realize that we had married too young and not necessarily for the right reasons. I understood now that I had been more enthusiastic about acquiring a family than a husband. And I was becoming a different person. All my life, I had lusted after a real education, but it had always seemed tantalizingly out of reach. I had no high school diploma, knew little of history or literature, and had never had a course in physics, chemistry, or mathematics. But in Paris I heard about a special program at the Sorbonne called the *année préparatoire.* People without high school diplomas could take a one-year course, and if they passed an exam at the end of the year, they could enter the Sorbonne proper. I enrolled, and, with a lot of effort—everything was conducted in French, after all—passed the exam. I decided I would study to become a clinical psychologist, which was not surprising given my penchant for introspection and my lifelong interest in other people's problems. I entered the Institute of Psychology, where I took classes with famous psychologists like Jean Piaget and Daniel Lagache. This was exciting, but, then, even walking down the venerable hallways at the Sorbonne and taking notes in lecture halls named after Richelieu, Michelet, and Descartes was a thrill. All in all, I felt like I had died and gone to heaven.

David was going through some changes of his own, too. He had come to the decision that he didn't really want to be a doctor, and in 1954 we went back to Israel for the summer. At the end of that time, matters came to a head. I returned to Paris to finish my studies, and David stayed behind. Over the course of the year, I became convinced that the marriage was over, and I asked him for a divorce. He agreed, and it was all arranged by a group of rabbis in Paris and carried out by mail.

I am happy to say that David and I have remained friends for the last fifty years and have gotten together on numerous occasions both in America and in Israel, where he became a press representative in the government. I guess this shows that our breakup wasn't exactly the stuff of a tragic Mouloudji song, but I have a confession to make: when all is said and done, I really don't believe that turbulent songs of passion, jealousy, and lover's torment offer the best models for conducting or ending relationships. Later—when I had become Dr. Ruth and had my own weekly radio show—I had a musical response for any caller who phoned in seeking advice about a relationship that was clearly going nowhere. I would make a signal to my engineer, and a song from *South Pacific* would come onto the airwaves: "I'm gonna wash that man right outa my hair— / And send him on his way." Far less romantic, but far more practical than anything you'd find in Mouloudji.

I had never heard of *South Pacific* or Rodgers and Hammerstein back then, of course, but in a pinch, it was Edith Piaf who came through for me, with a song called "Demain il fera jour." One door had closed, but another would open. My life would go on:

Tomorrow, it will be day.
It's when everything is lost
That everything begins.
Tomorrow it will be day.
After love,
Another love begins.
A young lad will come along whistling,
Tomorrow . . . for tomorrow
You will smile again,
Love again, suffer again,
Always.
Tomorrow it will be day.

Or as another of my favorite French songs had it more simply, "Tomorrow, it will be fine on the great road."

After my separation and divorce from David, I did a fair amount of dating. At one point I was very attracted to a Moroccan Orthodox Jewish student who I thought had eyes just like Mouloudji. I used to eat in a certain kosher restaurant just so I could be near him. Unfortunately, he never seemed particularly aware of my existence.

I had better luck with a good-looking young man named Dan, a French Jew who had lived on a kibbutz a few years before returning to Paris. We were in the midst of a wonderful love affair when one day, in 1956, I received a check from the West German government for five thousand marks–about fifteen hundred dollars–a reparation payment made to victims of Nazi war crimes who had not yet finished their education. I had made it a point never to seek out restitution from the Germans, for no cash payment could ever make up for what I had lost. Still, I was not about to refuse money that was right in front of me. On the spur of the moment, I decided that I would allow the German government to treat me to a well-deserved vacation. I would go to the United States and visit some friends from Heiden who had settled in New York, then go on to San Francisco, where my uncle Max, whom I hadn't seen since I was three years old, was living. At the end of the summer, I would go back to Israel, where I had planned to make my permanent home. Of course, I didn't want to do this traveling all on my own. I asked Dan to join in on the adventure, and he readily agreed.

What is it that they say about the best laid plans of mice and men? On our second day in New York, I was flipping through the pages of the *Aufbau*, the German Jewish newspaper, looking at the classified ads for lodging, when I saw another advertisement. The New School for Social Research was announcing a scholarship for a Nazi victim interested in pursuing a master's degree in sociology. I immediately decided to apply, and by the next day I had been informed that the scholarship was mine. I would stay in New York. "Non, je ne regrette rien."

I was twenty-seven years old, living in my fifth country, and trying to master my fifth language. I was a full-time student at the

New School, first studying to complete my B.A. requirements, then moving into the master's program, with never enough money to make ends meet, and working at a whole range of part-time jobs, cleaning houses for a dollar a day to start, conducting marketing research a bit later. Within a year, I discovered I was pregnant, and Dan and I married. My wonderful, wonderful daughter, Miriam, was born in 1957, but I'm afraid that Dan moved out of our lives a year later. Once again, a marriage ended. Dan and I divorced, and he returned to Europe. I was a single mother.

Until this point, I had seemed to absorb the music of my surroundings at each new stage of my life and in each new setting. Music colors my memories of Frankfurt, Heiden, Ayanot, Paris—but not of New York in those early years, and I don't know why, really. I say that it was because I was so busy raising my little girl, going to school, and working at a variety of jobs; I had no time to listen to American music. I say, too, that I had no money in those years; of course, I couldn't go to places where music might be played. But I'd never had money in Switzerland, Israel, or France, and I'd never *not* had to work overtime to make my way in the world. Maybe it's just that the music that was available to me in New York in the fifties didn't touch my soul. Maybe this time I really was a fish out of water.

And so, when I write about the music of that time, it's mostly about the things that I missed. This was the heyday of the American musical comedy. *My Fair Lady*, *Gypsy*, *The Music Man*, and a whole raft of other shows were playing on Broadway, just eight or nine miles south of the German Jewish enclave of

Washington Heights where I lived, but I didn't have the time or money to see any of them. Jazz clubs lined the streets of the west fifties, but they might as well have been on another planet for all I knew (and to tell the truth, I wouldn't have enjoyed them if I had gone; jazz has never been my thing). The folk revival was taking off in Greenwich Village, and this did percolate uptown just a bit; my good friend Al Kaplan—the man who loved Gilbert and Sullivan—would try to convince me that I was in a wonderful place by singing a song called "The Village of New York," by a folk group called the Easy Riders.

I look at lists of the top hits of 1956, 1957, 1958, 1959, and it's just one unfamiliar name after another. Nothing. You might think that the future Dr. Ruth would have been astounded by the gyrating sexuality of Elvis the Pelvis, the King of Rock 'n' Roll. It passed me right by. Did I ever hear him sing "Hound Dog," "Love Me Tender," "All Shook Up" on television or radio? I don't recall.

But I was making my way. I had loads of good friends, both from school and from my Washington Heights neighborhood, where I live to this day. I had an apartment at the time on Seaman Avenue, above Dyckman Street, and though I didn't have a lot in the way of furniture, I did have a phonograph. So what if I had nothing much to play on it? Every Friday night, after I'd put Miriam to bed, scores of people would come over, some bringing food, others something to drink, and others—most important—records. For the life of me, I can't remember any in particular, but we would spin platter after platter, and dance the night away. Waltzes, tangos, fox trots. I had my own salon at last, but without the conversation, and my very own bourgeois version of the Friday night dances on the kibbutz.

In the spring of 1961, some friends invited me to join them for a skiing weekend in the Catskills. I arranged for Miriam to stay with other friends in New Jersey, and off I went. There was one member of the group I hadn't known before, and as it happened,

we rode up the mountain on the ski lift together. We started to talk–and continued all day. He was quieter than I was (who isn't?), but a *Jecke* like me. He was an electrical engineer, and short and good-looking and unmarried. I took to him immediately. In the evening, back at the lodge, he pulled out a harmonica and played music that brought back a flood of warm memories. And now I will tell you something strange.

I have always said that the first piece he played was "Die Tyroler sind lustig," the song about the happy Tyroleans that I always associated with standing by the window in Frankfurt with my beloved grandmother at my side. It is only now, more than sixty years later, that I realize that the melody I heard back then is shared with another song, and one I will always connect with my separation from everything and everyone I held dear as a child: "Kommt ein Vogel geflogen." "Dear bird, fly on. . . . / I can't join you. / I must remain here."

But surely it was the song of the happy Tyroleans that Fred Westheimer was playing.

CHAPTER FIVE

If I can make it there . . .

Fred and I were married on December 10, 1961, and afterward I had to face a sobering realization: I would probably never go back to Israel to live. Fred liked the cold weather and the change of seasons, and though he was born in Germany, just as I was, he had lived in the United States for twenty years and considered himself very much an American. My life, too, was now here.

The next years were very busy but happy ones, filled with work, study, child rearing–and the music that Fred brought into our household. We didn't have a lot of extra money, but Fred made a solid living as an engineer, and for the first time in my life I felt reasonably secure financially. Fred, on the other hand, somehow always felt poor. He didn't begrudge this supposed fact; it was just the way he saw himself, and I always suspected that it was at least in part out of solidarity with his good friend Dale Ordes, who *really* didn't have much money. Dale was Fred's special music buddy, and when they got together they would take out their guitars, Fred would add his harmonica, and they would sing songs such as "Brother Can You Spare a Dime" and "Nobody Knows You When You're Down and Out" from the

Depression, songs of the Spanish Civil War, protest songs calling for social justice, and newly minted folk pieces like Pete Seeger's "Where Have All the Flowers Gone" and Bob Dylan's "Blowing in the Wind."

I loved sitting and listening to the two of them sing, though I always found one piece in their folk-revival repertoire particularly poignant, almost difficult to hear. This was "Leaving on a Jet Plane," written by the then relatively unknown John Denver and recorded with great success by Peter, Paul, and Mary in 1967. Why did this of all songs sadden me so? It was as if I didn't even register the assurances of the last verse, where the singer promises to return to the lover from whom he must part, or perhaps I simply couldn't believe that the matter was really within his control. I, too, had once been separated from the people I loved, not by plane, but by train, and despite their promises, had never seen them again:

Already, I'm so lonesome I could cry.

So kiss me and smile for me,
Tell me that you'll wait for me,
Hold me like you'll never let me go.
I'm leavin' on a jet plane.
I don't know when I'll be back again–
Oh babe, I hate to go.

Much more to my liking was Malvina Reynolds's biting satire of middle-class conformity, "Little Boxes":

And the people in the houses
All went to the university. . . .
And they came out all the same.
And there's doctors and lawyers
And business executives
And they're all made out of ticky tacky
And they all look just the same. . . .

And the boys go into business
And marry and raise a family
In boxes made of ticky tacky
And they all look just the same. . . .

Fred Westheimer avoided all traces of ticky tacky throughout his life, but meanwhile, he, too, was married and raising a family of his own—with my instrumental help! Fred had adopted Miriam right away, and in 1963 our son, Joel, was born. I was glad to observe, over the years, that Joel seemed to take after Fred rather than me in regard to musical ability and mechanical aptitude. Fred was certainly the dominant factor in our children's musical lives, and whenever we traveled anywhere as a family, the car would be filled with group singing. When the kids were little, it was usually the folk and protest songs that he loved—"If I Had a Hammer" or "We Shall Overcome." Then, at my insistence, we would sing some of the Israeli songs. To the relief of Fred, Miriam, and Joel, I would always let them sing the loudest.

As a girl, Miriam played the recorder (just like her mother!) and piano, but her real talent was in dance, especially Israeli folk dance. She became an accomplished choreographer, both in this country and in Israel, where she lived for several years before returning to New York. As for Joel, he followed in his father's guitar-playing path. He was–and is–really quite good, and when he was an undergraduate at Princeton, he and a friend performed professionally. I once went to see them play in a Greenwich Village coffeehouse, and they premiered a song of Joel's called "The Jewish Mother Blues," one of whose lines went, "I've got a mother who talks about certain things on the air." Joel eventually dropped his musical career in favor of one as a professor, but he still composes songs for special events and takes out his guitar at family gatherings. He gets everybody to sing, even me.

In 1970 I received a doctorate in education at Columbia University's Teachers College. It is a day I will always remember with pride. The degree represented the culmination of years of hard work, but still I had to pinch myself to be sure that it was for real. Hadn't I once been the child whose dream of going to school was made to seem so unreachable and whose impossible hope it was to become a kindergarten teacher? And now I was about to embark on a career as a college professor, with a first job at Lehman College in the Bronx, a branch of the City University of New York.

A few years later, so that I could better instruct high school teachers handling the sex education curriculum, I took some seminars in human sexuality. These led, eventually, to my being trained and licensed as a sex therapist and starting my own practice. One day I gave a speech to a group of community affairs managers from radio stations in the New York area about the need for improved sex education. As a direct follow-up, I was invited to be a guest on an interview program at WYNY Radio in New York. I taped the show on May 5, 1980, and that afternoon I got a call from Betty Elam, the community affairs manager at the station. Would I be interested in having my own program, every Sunday night between midnight and 12:15? I said yes without a moment of hesitation, and "Dr. Ruth" was born.

Betty said I would need two things: theme music and a name for the show. I was stumped on the first and went to the cantor of my synagogue in Washington Heights, Fred Herman. Within an hour he presented me with a recording of a baroque dance by an anonymous composer played on recorder and drum. I immediately felt it was perfect, both elegant and rhythmic—and rhythm is always related to sexuality (think of Ravel's *Bolero* and the way it is used in the movie *Ten*). I used the baroque theme on every radio show I did for the next ten years. I also needed a title for the show, and for this I sought my own Fred's advice. He suggested *Sexually Speaking*, and that was perfect, too.*

For the first show I merely gave a kind of mini-lecture on recent developments in the field of sex education, but I closed with a plea for people to write in with any questions. Sure

*For my 450 television shows, mostly on the Lifetime cable network, I had original music themes, commissioned under the able direction of my executive producer, John Lollos. I have a special attachment, though, to that first baroque piece.

enough, by the second week there was a stack of letters. For the first year, the show was a kind of audio Ann Landers column about sex. Then the program became popular enough to expand to an hour, move to ten o'clock on Sunday nights, and take phone calls. It was a sensation from the start and was quickly allotted an additional hour. At fifty-three years old, I was a celebrity.

I speak from firsthand experience when I say that fame is a strange phenomenon in the United States. One minute I was private citizen Ruth, known only to family and friends, and Dr. Westheimer to my circle of students, clients, and professional colleagues; the next I was a personality recognized by one and all as "Dr. Ruth." Practically overnight, my life changed in any number of ways—and most of them, contrary to what you might think, quite pleasant. Not a day goes by that I don't find myself thinking, "It's nice being Dr. Ruth"—and observing that in our culture it often seems much more useful to be famous than well educated.

One of the things I've most enjoyed about life as Dr. Ruth is being able to go to the theater and concerts whenever my schedule permits. Suddenly, I had the means to see every musical comedy on Broadway, including revivals of some of the shows I'd missed in the fifties and sixties, either because I wasn't in this country yet or couldn't afford to buy seats even in the "nosebleed" section. I've been privileged to be invited to many opening nights, and if I want tickets for a show that I've missed seeing at its premier, I can usually phone up for house seats and bypass months of waiting for tickets to the most popular shows (as I said, "It's nice being Dr. Ruth"). Given the chance to attend so many musicals, I found that I loved everything about them: the singing, the dancing, the stories, and the endings–which are usually happy. On the other hand, although I love going to the Metropolitan Opera for the grand experience of it, I am generally not as big a fan of opera. I tend to move quickly, and operas are too slow, and they so rarely turn out well! There are some, however, I do enjoy, even if they do end tragically. The music of *La Bohème* is so lush and the Parisian setting so loaded with associations for me that I'll suffer its story of star-crossed and consumptive passion any day. And I do love Mozart's *Magic Flute*, which delights me from start to finish, but especially when the bird-man Papageno finds a perfect match in his Papagena. I like to think that there is a perfect somebody out there for everyone–even if you are a feathery nonconformist.

I would say my favorite musical of all has to be Andrew Lloyd Webber's *Phantom of the Opera*. I must have seen it twenty times since it opened in 1988. Every time a friend expresses interest in seeing it, I offer to get him or her tickets–then I end up going, too. I love the theatricality, the haunting melodies, and the sheer sentimentality–and there's even a happy ending of sorts. My favorite song in the score is "Music of the Night"; the lyrics, by Charles Hart and Richard Stilgoe, suggest more than a little bit of music's power–and, not coincidentally, its close relationship to sexuality and love:

> Softly, deftly, music shall caress you,
> Hear it, feel it, secretly possess you.
> Open up your mind, let your fantasies unwind

In this darkness which you know you cannot fight,
The darkness of the music of the night.

For my seventieth birthday party, in 1998, my business associate Pierre Lehu secretly arranged for Rick Hilsabeck, a star of *Phantom* on Broadway, to come and serenade me with the song. He held me in his arms as he sang, as if I were Christine, the ingenue with whom he is romantically obsessed. Unquestionably, it was one of the highlights of my life as Dr. Ruth—maybe even of my life as Ruth K. Westheimer!

Part of being a celebrity, it sometimes seems, is having your own television talk show, and over the years I have presided over no fewer than three of them. I have had many musicians as guests, and some of them happened to be connected to the world of rock music. I was willing to talk to most anyone, especially after my producer, John Lollos, had briefed me about what subjects to cover (even when you're familiar with the guest's accomplishments, you won't have an interesting TV show if the only thing you can do is gush about what a marvelous and talented person he or she is; that's why producers interview the guests beforehand to get information from which special on-air moments can be constructed). But I'd never heard of most of the rock performers I interviewed, and there were times that my lack of familiarity surprised those who worked on the show. Once, Bianca Jagger was a guest, and I asked John who she was. He was not all that surprised that I didn't know her; after all, he and I had worked closely for so many years that he knew the depth of my ignorance when it came to pop culture. Even he was surprised, though, when I didn't react when he told me that she was the ex-wife of Mick Jagger. As far as I was concerned, the Rolling Stones didn't exist. Occasionally, though, John used my ignorance to his advantage. I would never have agreed to have Ozzy Osbourne on the program had I known that he was famous for biting off the head of a bat during a concert. But since I was unaware of his taste in onstage snacks, he and I had a wonderful interview. He was a funny and charming guest, and as we all know by now, he is a devoted family man.

One guest I most definitely *had* heard of was Itzhak Perlman, the violinist and conductor, whom I greatly admire and whom I've often seen perform in Israel and the United States. Before he appeared on the show, one of the co-producers, Marsha Lebby, did a pre-interview and discovered that Itzhak is a big fan of doo-wop music. With the cameras running, I asked him about it, and as soon as he said the word (or is it words?), out onto the stage came a doo-wop group. Not only did they sing to him, but they got him to sing with *them*. It was a wonderful moment, and it certainly wouldn't have happened if I hadn't become "Dr. Ruth."

I enjoyed the doo-wop, but not surprisingly, rock music isn't my thing. I do have a favorite band, however: U2. Truth be told, this is less because of their music than because I admire the humanitarian efforts of their lead singer, Bono, who puts his celebrity to good use, and because, for reasons I don't quite understand, they are big fans of *mine*. When they won a Grammy one year, Bono thanked a long list of people, one of whom was "Dr. Ruth." The next year, they asked me to record a radio commercial for their album *Zooropa.* And when they came to New York as part of their tour, I went to the concert with my administrative assistant, Cliff Rubin, who is also a rock musician. The best part was when U2, in front of 20,000 screaming fans, greeted me warmly as they walked off the stage. Not for the first time or the last, I thought to myself, "You've come a long way from Frankfurt am Main."

If I have to say what I like best about rock, it is that, like so many other kinds of music, past and present, it is intimately tied up with dance. As I've said before, I much prefer the forms of dancing where you touch and hold your partner, and I would be remiss if I didn't mention here that my husband Freddie did a fabulous polka. But rock-style dancing has its own charms: it's expressive, rhythmic, and often joyous. I will always remember the Democratic National Convention of 1992 in Madison Square Garden, which I covered for Nostalgia Television. When Bill Clinton's nomination was about to be announced, Pierre Lehu, his wife, Joanne, and I snuck to the front of the floor and stood with the Arkansas delegation. At the moment that Clinton's name was boomed out, thousands of balloons dropped from the ceiling, Fleetwood Mac's wonderful song "Don't Stop Thinking About Tomorrow" came on the loudspeaker system, and everybody in the Garden—on the podium and on the floor—started to boogie. I don't think I've ever witnessed so many people dance with so much joy.

People who know me are well aware that when the opportunity arises, I will take off my shoes and dance without giving it a second thought. When the music is infectious, people should get up and dance and not be self-conscious about being uncool or too old. I recently found myself once again at Madison Square Garden, this time for an Elton John concert, and sitting up front with the VIPs. Some of the songs just made me want to get up and dance, but the people all around me were as still as stones. Finally, I stood up and grabbed a man who was sitting in the row behind me and forced him to dance with me in the aisle. I'm sure he was a big shot, but I was too busy dancing to ask his name.

Once when I was out to dinner with my friends Fred Howard and Bonnie Kaye, Fred said he would contribute a sizable check to a documentary I was planning on Ethiopian Jews if I would get up and dance on a table! If he thought I would chicken out, he was sorely mistaken. I looked around the restaurant, found the tallest and best-looking waiter there, and called him over. I took off my shoes, had him hoist me on the table and asked him to hold my hand (so I wouldn't fall off the table) as I twirled around. Another time, I was at a big fund-raiser where Zubin Mehta was conducting the dance music. That was thrill enough, but as I was moving around the dance floor with someone or other–I forget who–Mehta's manager tapped me on the shoulder. "The Maestro wishes to dance with you," he said. I dropped my companion, the Maestro handed over his baton to a colleague, and away we went. But the very best dancing of my life was in a Jerusalem hotel. I was there with my friend Daniel Schwartz for a meeting of the Young Presidents' Organization, a wonderful association that brings together young business leaders from seventy-five nations around the world. A professional ballroom dancer from China, the husband of one of the delegates, asked me onto the dance floor. I guess he knew that I like to take control, because he inquired first if I would let him lead. I promised I'd let him try, and I guess I succeeded, because I've never danced waltzes or tangos like that!

As easy and as much fun as it is for me to dance, I still have anxieties about singing in public. But being Dr. Ruth has helped me confront and, to a degree, overcome some of those feelings. Admittedly, it's being Dr. Ruth that has gotten me into the unlikely situations where I have to sing in public in the first place. Once, PBS broadcast an AIDS benefit from the Metropolitan Opera. It was on a Sunday night, which was when my radio show aired, so after making some opening remarks at the benefit, I had to hop into a waiting car to dash twenty blocks downtown to Rockefeller Center to do my show. As soon as I was off the air, I once again jumped into the car and went back up to Lincoln Center to the opera house. I got there just in time to join everyone on stage in the last song. It was "The Best of Times" from the show *La Cage aux Folles*, and as tone-deaf Ruth Westheimer stood there singing on the stage of the Metropolitan Opera, I remember thinking how wonderfully unpredictable life can be. And I remember, too, thinking about my supervisors from the kindergarten in Paris—the ones who despaired over my singing limitations—and wishing they could see me now. At the end of the evening, I was given the coat of many colors that had been worn on stage, signed by many of the celebrities who had been a part of the show. As I said, it's nice being Dr. Ruth.

Another unlikely singing appearance was little more than a

cameo but lots of fun. Every year the mayor of New York stars in a show that pokes fun at himself and others in city government. Mayor Ed Koch was and still is a friend of mine. At one of these performances during his term, he put on a version of *Little Shop of Horrors*, one of the stars of which is Audrey, a man-eating plant. When the mayor introduced this plant to the audience and it opened its mouth, I popped out. Naturally it brought the house down.

In 1995 I was asked to appear in a benefit performance of *Pippin*, in the role of Berthe, the title character's grandmother. She has only one number in the show, "No Time at All," and it can be talked, rather than sung, and so I agreed. In one regard, the part wasn't much of a stretch for me, my non-singing abilities notwithstanding. After all, what Berthe does is to give advice. I loved the song, and thought the words were ones I could practically have written myself (though not nearly so wittily as the composer and lyricist Stephen Schwartz):

> I've never wondered if I was afraid
> When there was a challenge to take
> I never thought about how much I weighed
> When there was still one piece of cake. . . .
> Oh, it's time to start livin'
> Time to take a little from the world we're given
> Time to take time, for Spring will turn to Fall
> In just no time at all.

Still, it was a song, and I was going to be out there on a stage in front of a theater full of strangers. I rehearsed endlessly with the musical director and was so nervous about missing a cue and looking professional that I wouldn't let any of my family come see the performance. But the trio of singers who were my chorus led me through my paces perfectly, and when I was done, I was given a standing ovation. That taught me a lesson: I have invited my children and grandchildren to every performance I've given since then.

That experience also helped me understand that in some contexts "talking" a song can work just as well as singing it. It worked for Rex Harrison, didn't it? My next experiment was on a celebrity karaoke show put on by VH1. I always like being on VH1 or MTV because it provides an opportunity to get my message about safer sex across to a younger audience. Pierre Lehu assured me that the song he selected for me, "A Touch of Gray" by the Grateful Dead, could be spoken. And so it could. Best of all, this was at a time when I had let my own hair go gray, so I could point to it when I was performing. Later, the people of Clairol called me to do commercials for their Herbal Essence line, and I was "forced" to go back to being a blonde. In truth, I like it, but I enjoyed having gray hair for a time and got a kick out of singing on television to commemorate it.

I have had a number of offers to appear professionally in musicals, all of which I've declined. As you know, I can't hold a tune, and while I love going to the theater, I certainly don't want to tie myself down to going to the same one night after night. Even so, I was certainly flattered when Tommy Tune, who is at least twice as tall as I am, offered me the opportunity to play his mother in a revival of *Bye Bye Birdie*, and I was amused at the prospect of being the narrator in *The Rocky Horror Picture Show* on Broadway for a week. There was, in fact, a much less painful way for me to get onto the musical stage, and it was one that allowed me to sit back in my seat in the audience while watching my own Broadway debut! This was in William Finn and James Lapine's brilliant *Falsettos*, when the character named Mendel, a psychiatrist, wonders why he can't let himself be happy. Out come three giant singing heads to nag at his conscience: Freud, Jung, and . . . Dr. Ruth! "Why doncha feel all right for the rest of your life?" we sing in unison. Someone had tipped me off about this in advance, but I didn't mention anything to my executive producer, John Lollos, my companion for the evening. I don't know what I enjoyed more, seeing the singing Dr. Ruth on stage in such august company or watching John's reaction to it all.

Probably the most memorable performance of my not especially brilliant career came about because of my love of chocolate. I was on my way to my hair stylist, Richard Stein, and I stopped at the Teucher chocolate shop around the corner for a chocolate fix. A woman approached me saying that she wanted me to narrate a piece she was preparing. I was there with Pierre Lehu, and he gave her his card so that she could get in touch with me with further details. I'm sure that if I had not already performed in *Pippin* and gotten my feet wet, I would ultimately have turned down the offer she was about to make and would never have been nominated for a Grammy. But I'm getting ahead of myself.

The woman's name was Connie Emmerich, and she was and still is the artistic director and pianist for a chamber music group called An Die Musik. She had commissioned composer Bruce Adolph to set "Little Red Riding Hood" to music. My job was to read the text in counterpoint to the music that the group played between the blocks of spoken narration. Again I was nervous about missing a cue, but when we performed the piece at Merkin Hall, by Lincoln Center, all I had to do was keep my eye on the lead violinist, who would give me the high sign when I was to begin reading. Everything worked so well that I agreed to be the narrator again, this time for a version of "Goldilocks and the Three Bears" the following year.

I performed with An Die Musik several other times, including once at a concert series produced by Rockefeller University. Half of the audience members were doctors in their white coats, and I was so impressed that I kept looking out at the audience instead of watching the violinist, and as a result almost missed one of my cues.

Connie thought that the performances went so well that we should record them for posterity. I agreed, mainly because I thought it would be nice to have a souvenir, and never imagining that the resulting CD would lead to very much. But Larry Kramen, the head of our label, Newport Records, entered the recording into competition and it ended up being nominated for a Grammy Award–in the spoken-word category, of course. I didn't know this was even a possibility, so let me tell you, when I found out, no one was more surprised than I was. But surprise or no, once nominated, I wanted to win. I did some checking around and found that the best course of action was to put an ad in Billboard, the music industry trade publication. Not wanting to leave anything to chance, I made an appointment and went over to Billboard myself in order to talk to the people in charge.

As you might imagine, the people who work at Billboard are used to seeing all manner of rock stars. But while I was told that they are blasé when famous musicians walk the halls, they made a big fuss over me, lining up outside the conference room we were in, waiting to get my autograph. I turned out to be a hit, and because of that, not only was my ad given special placement, but they even put my picture on the cover, along with U2, James Taylor, Alicia Keys, Don Henley, and John Mellencamp. Not bad for someone who can't sing or play a note–sometimes it's positively *strange* being Dr. Ruth.

I would like to be able to tell you that the quality of the recording and the publicity campaign that I mounted were enough to win the Grammy, but they weren't, and I returned from the award ceremony in Los Angeles empty-handed (except for a terrific goody bag of freebies). But if we had to lose, I was glad that it was to Tom Chapin, a friend of mine, who had convinced me to do a duet with him on his previous album, "This Pretty Planet." By the way, the song I performed with Tom (I say performed because once again I really spoke my lines rather than sang them) was very cute:

> There's two kind of seagulls:
> He-gulls and she-gulls.

He-gulls like she-gulls
And that's why there's seagulls.

There's two kinds of penguins:
Ladyquins and menquins.
Ladyquins flip for menquins
And that's why there's penguins.

Most creatures come in pairs.
That's the way they mingle.
One kind only would be lonely.
It takes two to tingle.

There's two kinds of peoples:
He-ples and she-ples.
He-ples like she-ples.
And she-ples like he-ples.
And that's why there's me-ples,
And you-ples and peoples.

As you can see, the topic was right up my alley, and it also gave me the opportunity to appear on a CD that I could proudly give to my grandchildren.

All these experiences are a lot of fun, but music is most meaningful to me when I am sitting in the concert hall, not standing on the stage, and when the music being performed is classical. Since my husband Fred died, in 1997, I have become an inveterate concertgoer. Sometimes I plan in advance and sometimes, if it turns out that I have a free evening, I will just go over to Lincoln Center, see what is on for that evening, and buy a ticket to whatever concert is taking place.

On one level, concertgoing offers an opportunity to go out with good friends and do something worthwhile, and not be a boring German Jewish widow sitting around over coffee and cake and having the same conversations every week. But it's more than that. By myself in the concert hall, I don't have to talk, I don't have to be "on." Thanks to awful Fräulein Riesenfeld from Heiden and my relative Liesel from Jerusalem, I have trained myself to concentrate on the moment, without being aware of anything else. I consciously sit and open the pores of my soul to the music. I cannot tell you when a movement starts or ends, I cannot tell you when the piano or violins come in, and, quite frankly, if you ask me the next day I very often cannot tell you the name of the piece or even the composer. But it is a powerful and cleansing experience nevertheless. It's like letting a wave come near me but not overpower me.

Concerts are occasions of delight for me, and one of my greatest pleasures is watching the conductor. Often, I am reminded of a friend's comment that a good conductor looks like he or she is making love to the orchestra. I certainly feel that way watching the brilliant Zubin Mehta, who has become a friend in recent years. I would have to say that one of the highlights of my life was sitting in Zubin's box at the New York Philharmonic and knowing that as he walked off the stage, he would look up at me and acknowledge my presence.

I recently asked him about the common thread of his many years in music—he has been a conductor in Israel, Bosnia, Norway, Japan, India, Canada, the United States, and Germany—and he said his wanderings stemmed from an "obsession": "I cannot stop. I have this will to bring out the music, to convince people to bring out their best." When I asked him about the sexual communication I sensed between him and the orchestra, he laughed and said, "It has nothing to do with sex. But it is all about communication, and the eyes are a great part of it. I have constant eye contact with the musicians—if I don't, I am very upset about it. And you can tell that you're working well with them when, in concert, the music takes on an indescribable dimension that does not happen at rehearsals."

He paused. "If you want to talk about sexual communication in music, the most incredible example I saw in my life was between Daniel Barenboim and his wife, Jacqueline du Pré [the cellist, who died in 1987], when they played a Beethoven or a Brahms sonata. Of course, nobody was thinking of sex. When I heard them play, I always thought of a painting by Chagall that shows a young couple floating in space together. That's what they sounded like. They were suddenly in one mind, and they didn't realize it."

Zubin also gave me some insight into why Mozart's *Eine kleine Nachtmusik* is my favorite single piece, by the way. "It is perfection in sound, when you think that Mozart wrote it from beginning to end, without making one mistake," he said. "In its style, it is the perfect circle of a composer. The Germans believe in symmetry, and this is the perfect example of symmetry in music."

Another pleasure is following the careers of particular musicians. I have already mentioned my affection for Itzhak Perlman, both as a violinist and as a person. I also have a special place in my heart for the young cellist Inbal Megiddo, who was born in Israel and now lives in the United States. I first saw her at the Yitzhak Rabin memorial concert at Madison Square Garden in 1995, where she played a solo piece called *Kaddish*, after the Jewish prayer for the dead. When I saw her playing all alone, in front of those thousands of people, I thought to myself, "That is a very talented and gutsy young lady." She was a Yale sophomore at the time, and when we spoke after the concert, she asked if I would speak at the college. I agreed without hesitation. Two years later I went to Yale as promised. After dinner at Calhoun College, we crossed the street to attend a concert in one of Yale's churches. The only performers were cellists–Inbal and about twenty others. Since then, she has performed as a soloist with several orchestras, including the Prague Chamber Orchestra and the Boston Classical Orchestra, and given performances at the Kennedy Center in Washington and Carnegie and Alice Tully Halls in New York. I have nothing but admiration for someone with so much talent, artistry, and persistence.

Other concerts that stick in my memory are those of my grandchildren. Obviously these are not of the professional quality of the ones I've been writing about, but to a grandmother, they are even more precious. My grandson Ari plays the clarinet, and I've attended concerts of his school orchestra. And my two little granddaughters, Leora (Miriam's daughter) and Michal (Joel's), love to put on shows when they get together.

Believe me, there's no better entertainment in the whole wide world to a proud grandparent. Just days before I wrote these words, Joel and his wife, Barbara, had their second child and first son, Benjamin Manfred Leckie Westheimer (Manfred was my husband Fred's formal first name). I immediately flew up to Ottawa, Canada, to see all of them. Let me tell you, what sweet music the sound of Benjamin's voice was!

The apartment building in which I live is at the western edge of Manhattan Island, with windows facing in that direction. Directly below me as I look out is the Hudson River and, across it, the New Jersey Palisades. The George Washington Bridge is just to the left, and if I crane my neck a bit, I have the Tappan Zee Bridge to my right. The sunlight pours in during the day and the view is fabulous at any hour, but I love it especially when the sun sets over the river, or at night, when the bridge is lit up to look like a giant glowing erector set project. With a view like this, how could I ever think of moving?

And when I turn away from the window to look at the view *inside*, I know there's another reason why I'll never move. How could I ever tackle the happy tumult of books, papers, and objects that are here? There is no trace of the bourgeois *Jeckish* order of Liesel's apartment in Jerusalem that I longed for so many years ago. I'm surrounded by clutter, and I confess I love it this way.

Peeking out from beneath the papers that sometimes seem to cover every surface are turtles, I don't know how many, in every size and every style, made of clay or wood, metal or stone. Some are quite beautiful, others you might call kitsch, but I collect them for myself, and people give them to me, and the turtle population increases. Why turtles? Think about it. The turtle can stay in its shell and be safe and boring, but it will never get anywhere unless it sticks its neck out. And that's the story of Ruth Westheimer.

In my study is one of my most prized possessions, a dollhouse completely fitted out with furniture, china, and carpets. A radio stands in the miniature parlor. The dining room table is set for a family dinner. It is hard to explain to my granddaughters Leora and Michal that the dollhouse is off limits to them when they come to visit, that this is one thing that is grandma's alone. They are still too young to note or understand that everything in the dollhouse is true to the period of the 1930s. Is this the dollhouse I would have had if my own childhood had not been interrupted? Or is it the very home I feel I lost? It is there like a Chinese puzzle, one small home I've made but can never inhabit, standing inside the larger one in which I live.

And then, there are my music boxes. Some of them are extravagances, some quite simple, but I make no distinctions between them; I am not interested in their retail value but their emotional capital.

One plays the tune of "Here Comes the Bride," and as I listen, the familiar melody makes me smile. I really do believe in the institution of marriage, though I never thought I would enter it quite as often as I did. Clearly, I struck gold on my third try, and I was very, very fortunate in that. Will I have a fourth opportunity? I'm not ruling it out.

I have two snow globes, one a souvenir from Washington, D.C., that plays "The Battle Hymn of the Republic," another with the Manhattan skyline and the anthem to all that is possible in "New York, New York." I *have* made it here, and certainly in ways I couldn't have imagined when I think of the associations I have with the next music box. This one is in the form of a miniature sewing machine, with a foot pedal that moves up and down as it plays a melody from *Swan Lake.* It was a gift, and it always makes me laugh. In 1956, when I first came to America, I passed a store window in which were displayed Singer sewing machines, available for purchase on installments of one dollar a week. With my imperfect English, I thought this was the funniest thing. "Who knows?" I asked Dan, "Perhaps I'll need to make my living by singing and sewing at the same time?" I bought one and still have it. It wasn't musical, but the miniature is.

I have two boxes that play "Edelweiss." I know, of course, that this is really a Broadway tune from a show set in Austria, but it reminds me of my beloved Swiss Alps anyway. One of the two has little wooden figures of children dancing around its surface like the small children I took care of at Heiden so long ago. The other is in the form of a tiny Swiss chalet, and it stands next to a larger, nonmusical chalet I bought years back on a trip to Switzerland, much to Fred's consternation. We were hiking in the mountains and I saw the model for sale in a shop at the foot of a trail. It cost the equivalent of $70, a fortune for me at the time, and though it was expensive and completely non-functional, I had to have it, and have it *now.* I don't know what came over me, but I was sure that if I waited until we trekked back down the mountain, somebody else would snatch it out from under me. So I bought it on the spot and lugged it around all day, and now the big chalet and the little chalet sit side by side on a table in my living room.

But without a doubt, the most beautiful music box in my collection is the carousel with hand-carved horses, a gift from Miriam and her husband, Joel Einleger. I confess now that I am not so fond of the melody it plays. Wind it up and the horses prance around in a circle to the tune of Andrew Lloyd Webber's "Memories." I've dredged up a lot of memories for this book, of course, but you must understand that in some fundamental way, this is counter to my nature. I never want to be someone who sits in her rocking chair dwelling only on the past. I choose to live in the here and now and to move forward without stopping.

On May 11, 2002, along with a few dozen other honorees, I was presented with the Ellis Island Medal of Honor. This award has been presented annually since 1986 by the National Ethnic Coalition of Organizations (NECO) and, according to the organization, is "designed to pay homage to the immigrant experience, as well as individual achievement." I was very honored to be selected. Previous recipients include four presidents and Generals Colin Powell and Norman Schwarzkopf. I did not come to this country through Ellis Island, but the symbolism of the place is extraordinarily resonant. It represents for generations of immigrants and their children the fact that almost *all* Americans come from somewhere else.

When I left Germany in 1939, I was given what was called a

"Nansen passport," an identity card invented in 1922 by the Norwegian explorer and statesman Fridtjof Nansen, first issued by the League of Nations to stateless refugees, and eventually honored by governments in fifty-two countries. Later, after the state of Israel was formed, I became an Israeli citizen. For my first few years in this country, I thought of myself as an Israeli student, albeit a rather old one, completing her education before going back to Israel for the rest of her life. (I even spoke Hebrew with Miriam before English, and her first words were in Hebrew.) It was only after marrying Fred in 1961 that I came to the realization that I would never go back to Israel to live. So, in 1965, I boned up on the Consitution, the Bill of Rights, and the system of checks and balances and took the examination to become a citizen. I passed and have been happy and proud to be an American ever since.

The 2002 ceremonies started with an ecumenical service at St. Patrick's Cathedral, on Fifth Avenue. We were ushered to the front row. As I've said, I love being in churches, and St. Patrick's is especially grand, but there was one problem. I didn't realize that there is a little bench where Catholics kneel to pray, and the iron rod gave me a cut in my leg. I thought to myself, "This is the punishment a Jewish woman gets for being in church."

Fortunately, the rest of the day went without further mishap or injury. After a lunch uptown, we were taken to Ellis Island for the award ceremony. This was particularly notable because it was the first event to be held on the island since the terrible events of September 11, 2001. The ceremony was full of military pomp, with the presentation of the flag and soldiers saluting in all their regalia. A Marine band and a military orchestra both played a selection of patriotic songs and marches, and an a capella group of thirty soldiers serenaded the other honorees and me.

How far I had come from Switzerland, where I sang the patriotic songs with all my heart but at the same time knew that they didn't really apply to me! Now, I was not only accepted–I was being celebrated. I could sing "God Bless America" with no ambivalence, and not even with any concern about hitting the wrong note. At the same time, I felt an undeniable sadness. As the music swelled around me, I thought about what had happened just across New York Harbor only eight months before and also about the violence in Israel, where it appeared that the Israelis and Palestinians would never be able to live together in harmony. My life, I thought, has been a kind of thread, woven between periods of war and peace. Although I took some comfort from the sight of the soldiers that day, knowing that they would be willing and able to fight if called upon, I prayed, too, that my children and grandchildren and I would not see another war and all the horrors that it would bring.

These were my thoughts, and as I stood there, I thought, too, that things had come full circle, always to the accompaniment of anthems and patriotic songs. As a child, I felt myself to be a true German and am reminded of how wrong I was whenever I hear the lovely and painful national hymn. In Switzerland, I made a kind of deal to borrow Swiss patriotism and sang the associated songs with gusto, all the while knowing deep down that it was on a temporary basis. I sang wholeheartedly in Israel, but that, too, turned out to be temporary. Sitting in the Ellis Island reviewing stand, watching the spectacular Grucci fireworks explode above the Statue of Liberty and New York Harbor, to the tune of "The Star-Spangled Banner," I knew in my heart that this music was mine, that I had finally made my last stop.

Coda

As you know, my late husband Fred was the musical one in our marriage. He sang beautifully and played the guitar, harmonica, and piano. It was Fred's doing that our daughter, Miriam, learned the piano, too; and our son, Joel, got his musical talent from Fred, not from me, that's for sure. Always, it was Fred who was responsible for filling our home with music, and it is to his memory that I dedicate this book.

A better husband than Fred no woman ever had. He thought I could accomplish just about whatever I set my mind to do, but if truth be told, if he were alive today, I'm sure he'd be skeptical about this particular project of mine. As I write these pages, I can hear his voice clearly, talking to my editor. "What's the matter with you?" he would ask. "If you wanted someone in the family to write about music, why didn't you come to me? *She's* always said that she doesn't care all that much for music. And I hate to say it, but I really don't think she knows very much about it either."

But this time you're wrong, Freddie. I see now that I've cared all along. And in my own way, I guess I do know quite a lot after all.

Author's note

When I first began thinking about this book, I assumed it would be a fun project, but it has turned out to be a very meaningful one as well. I had no idea at the start how important a role music has played in my life. When it actually came time to explore the musical connections to my past, though, I discovered many memories that would otherwise probably have disappeared completely. A good number of these were sad, to be sure, but most of what I remembered was very positive. Music has a way of lifting your spirits, and those times when music has played an important role in my life have tended to be happy ones.

But enough about me. That's right. At this late point in the book, I'd like to turn from being Ruth Westheimer, autobiographer, to take on my better-known role of Dr. Ruth, advice giver. You see, if this process of discovering the role of music in *my* life proved so valuable to *me*, I know that looking for the music in *your* life will be just as valuable to *you*. I'd even go so far as to say invaluable. Since you are probably not a refugee, you probably possess many more mementos of your early life than I do, most importantly photographs–maybe even more photographs and videos than you know what to do with. These can obviously trigger many memories, but music, like math, is processed on the left side of your brain, while visual stimuli are processed on the right side. And while I haven't done any scientific studies, from what I was able to observe in my own case, I believe that using music to trigger recollection brings up a different view of those memories from what you would otherwise have. You may well summon up emotions that you couldn't by simply looking at a picture, especially as, when listening to music, you tend to focus inwardly. You may even close your eyes, so that you relive these experiences in a completely different, nonvisual way.

So what I'm suggesting is that you follow the same path that I did. Search your memory banks for the pieces of music that were playing at various times in your life. Then, listen to those pieces. If you can't find actual recordings, at least hum the melodies to yourself. See if the words come back to you. Then sit back and experience the memories each tune evokes. I guarantee you that you'll find the time very well spent.

And for those of you who are more adept at using electronic gadgets than I am—which is just about everybody!—I would even go so far as to suggest that you make a CD or tape of "the greatest hits of your life." In other words, construct your own musical autobiography. Include songs from your childhood as well as those that you associate with major events in your life. Some of these may be obvious, such as your wedding song; others may have significance only to you. There may even be songs that will bring very private moments flooding back to you, like the early days of a first love. That's an odd thing about listening to music—though others around you may hear the same song, its meaning to you will be unique.

Making such a recording will lead you to some of the very same places in which I found myself when putting together this book, and I know you'll find the experience just as significant and rewarding as I did. Moreover, any time you like, you'll be able to play this recording, either from beginning to end or jumping around. Close your eyes, let the notes float into your brain, and relive some of the most precious times of your life.

Acknowledgments

In addition to the individuals mentioned in this book, I would like to "sing" the praises of Jerry Singerman, editor extraordinaire, who initiated the idea of this volume; Ben Yagoda, the excellent writer with whom I have collaborated on a number of books; and Pierre Lehu, my superb "minister" of communications for the past twenty-two years. I also want to add my special thanks to Erica Ginsburg, Rebecca Rich, and other members of the staff of the University of Pennsylvania Press and to Fred Behrend, David Best, M.D., Mark Blechner, Ph.D., Esther Coopersmith, Mary Cuadrado, Ph.D., Marsha Bryan Edelman, Ed.D., Robert Freedman, Murray Horwitz, Steven Kaplan, Ph.D., Robert Krasner, M.D., Marga and Bill Kunreuther, Lou Lieberman, Ph.D., Sanford Lopater, Ph.D., Vernon Mosheim, Cantor Henry Rosenblum, Cliff Rubin, Daniel Schwartz, Amir Shaviv, Jeffrey Tabak, Esq., Malcolm Thomson, Gary Tinterow, and Greg Willenborg. My greatest thanks go to my family, Miriam Westheimer, Ed.D., and Joel Einleger, M.B.A., Joel Westheimer, Ph.D., and Barbara Leckie, Ph.D., and my four terrific grandchildren, Ari, Leora, Michal, and the newest arrival, Benjamin Manfred Leckie Westheimer. Their giggles are the sweetest music to my ears.